HARVEY HOUSES
of TEXAS

Historic Hospitality from the Gulf Coast to the Panhandle

ROSA WALSTON LATIMER

THE
History
PRESS

Published by The History Press
Charleston, SC 29403
www.historypress.net

First published 2014

Manufactured in the United States

ISBN 978.1.62619.524.0

Library of Congress CIP data applied for.

*This book is dedicated to my daughter, Lara, the
ever-present joy of my life*

and

*In loving memory of my sweet Dr. Bell, a remarkably
generous and wise man.*

CONTENTS

Contents

ACKNOWLEDGEMENTS

During the process of researching and writing this book, when someone, often a stranger, was helpful and interested in the project, I would think, "I've got to remember to include them in my acknowledgements!" Unfortunately, my mental notes didn't always evolve into written notes. I am certain I have forgotten the names of individuals who were supportive and those who shared an obscure nugget of Fred Harvey information with me. Thank you to all of you, collectively, who pushed this project along and helped me make it a reality.

I am especially indebted to Dana Smith, who provided sincere support when my idea for this book was in its infancy. She is still reassuring after many years, recently telling me, "The story needs to be told." Thank you, Dana!

Thanks, also, to Susan Lake, who many years ago took a plastic tub full of information and organized it into a form that allowed me to move forward.

I appreciate very much the financial support for research funded by two Post, Texas charitable organizations: the Maxine Durrett Earl Foundation and E.A. Franklin Trust.

Susan McGlothlin and the fine staff at the Cline Library, University of Northern Arizona, provided great, professional assistance throughout this process. Others who helped my research efforts were: Cindy Wallace, Amarillo, Texas Public Library; Art Gray, Gray's Studio, Amarillo; Wes Reeves, president, Amarillo Historical Preservation Foundation; Lisa Hanbury, River Valley Pioneer Museum, Canadian, Texas; Phyllis McPherson, Mollie Mims and Christy Norton, Layland Museum, Cleburne, Texas; Nikki Diller, Galveston

County Museum, Galveston, Texas; Judy Smith, Ice House Museum, Silsbee, Texas; Sue Davis, Jolene Fondy, Squeaky and Sandy Self, Slaton Railroad Heritage Association, Slaton, Texas; Skipper Murray, Somerville Historical Museum, Somerville, Texas; Barbara Keeney, assistant librarian, County/City Library, Sweetwater, Texas; Pioneer City-County Museum, Sweetwater; and Chris Godbold, Fort Bend County Museum Association, Richmond, Texas.

I could not have had better guides through the history of El Paso, Texas, than Patricia Bevel Kiddney and Pres Dehrkoop. These ladies organized and lead the organization Harvey Girls of El Paso, Texas, and are dedicated, knowledgeable and great fun.

Thank you and my sincere appreciation to Christen Thompson, my editor at The History Press, for her wise instruction and kind patience.

To Michael McMillan, I simply say, "Wow!" This man's response to an e-mail from a stranger (me) inquiring about Texas Harvey House images was phenomenal. I'll always remember the day that Michael was traveling in the far northern United States and found a place to upload images from his collection for me to use in this book. His knowledge of Harvey Houses throughout the United States is impressive. Anyone interested in preserving history should be thankful for folks like Michael.

Thank you, also, to my friends Jane Lindsay and Melissa Morrow. Jane, at the most unlikely time in her life, was the catalyst for me to push through with this project. Melissa's salient wisdom mixed with a keen sense of humor was often the voice in my head when the going got rough. You are both wonderfully unique and inspirational friends.

There are more special friends who have supported me in many ways for many years and thus brought me to this happy point in my life: Kathy Beach, Debbie Line, Lee and Marsha Norman, Mary Norman and Jim and Janice Plummer. I'd also like to thank the Post Public Library staff: Peggy Ashley and Linda Collazo, Sammy and Judy Ribble, Sammie Rodgers, Gary and Janet Schwantz, Patsy Lee Stephenson, Sue Swinson and Billie Williams, as well as my awesome extended family, the Utah Bells. I love you!

I am particularly thankful for the nine wonderful years I shared with "His Happiness," whose confidence and love are with me in spirit every day. I am so very fortunate to be among those who were touched by his love and optimistic enthusiasm.

And, finally, but with extreme enthusiasm I say, "Thank you!" to my daughter and very best friend, Lara, who daily shows me what sincere grace and kindness look like. Thank you for your encouragement and understanding. It is wonderful to have you in my life, and I love you, too!

INTRODUCTION

The week I graduated from high school, I received a large envelope with an out-of-state postmark. The name on the return address was "Balmanno." This name had never been spoken in our house, but before I was adopted, it was my family name. My adopted mother laid the envelope on my desk, silently giving her permission for me to read the contents.

The long letter inside, from my biological uncle, provided a wonderful family connection for me. Written in handwriting almost identical to my own, Uncle Bill told stories about every branch in our family tree. The paragraphs about my grandparents particularly captured my attention.

Gertrude Elizabeth McCormick met my grandfather William Alexander Balmanno in 1913 while she was working as a Harvey Girl in New Mexico. When William was twelve years old, he left his family on the Island of Mauritius in the Indian Ocean to work on whaling ships. At the age of twenty-nine, he and a friend quit their whaling days in Vera Cruz, Mexico, and decided to walk to California. On the way, in Rincon, New Mexico, William took a job with the Santa Fe Railroad to earn money to finish his trip.

My grandmother, an orphan who finished nursing school in Philadelphia, wanted to go to Alaska (looking for adventure, I suppose). She reasoned that working as a Harvey Girl would be a good start as it afforded the opportunity to transfer to different locations, all the way to California. Her first assignment was at the lunch counter in the Harvey House in Rincon, where she met William. They married three months later and spent the rest of their lives in New Mexico.

Harvey Girls Marie Olsen and Mabel Eubank in the Sunday, all-white uniforms required at the Harvey House in Union Station, Galveston, Texas. *Courtesy of Raymond Saenz.*

My uncle seemed quite proud of his mother's ties to the Harvey Houses built along the Santa Fe Railroad. He also assumed that I knew the story of the Harvey Girls and their strong influence on the settling of the West. I had no idea what he was talking about, but I wanted to know more about these Harvey Girls. I knew if I learned about them, I would also learn about my grandmother, a woman I last saw when I was two years old.

Thus began my research about Harvey Girls, the Harvey Houses where they worked and Fred Harvey, the man who advertised for "educated women of good character" to come west to work. Initially, of course, my personal interest was in my grandparents and New Mexico Harvey Houses. After a time, I realized that very little had been documented about the Harvey Houses that were stopping points for passenger trains as they rumbled across my home state of Texas. I began to focus my research on Texas Harvey Houses.

Lesley Poling-Kempes stated in the introduction to her book, *The Harvey Girls: Women Who Opened the West,* that the history of the Southwest would be incomplete without the story of the Harvey Girls. I believe the same is true for Texas history.

I was fortunate to spend time with some former Texas Harvey Girls and experience firsthand their energetic, adventuresome personalities, still evident after many years. Some shared their experiences in wonderful, handwritten letters. Family history, photos and memories were provided to me by family

Dear Mr Latimer
My mother was a Harvey Girl in the late 1920's and early 1930's Her name is Leona Woods Moore of Somerville, Texas. Her Story was on The Edge of Texas in the mid 1980s
She started working at the Harvey House in Temple in 1929 She was a dining room waitress and counter waitress also. Her Dispenser was Bertha Hartman. In 1929 she was transferred to Galveston. One year later she was transferred to Slaton's Harvey lunch room and worked for Mr Ed Bowman. She worked in Slaton 3 years until 1932 when she went to Grand Canyon for 2 years. In 1934 she went to Brownwood and then to Somerville in 1935 where she met and married my father Thomas L Moore, who was a Switchman for the Santa Fe.
She had many interesting pictures and memorabilia from Harvey Days and has donated some things to the museum here. She is 87 years old and still likes to talk about Harvey Days.
Sincerely
Carol Moore

Personal letter to author detailing the Harvey Girl career of Leona Woods More. *Author's collection.*

members. The majority of the women I spoke with, most of whom were well over eighty years of age, still had an abundance of energy and had remained far more active than many other women their age. Former Harvey Girl Erna Koen Johnson wrote, "I now live in a retirement home—am busy at age 90 years and life is good to me."

As I learned more about Harvey Girls and Harvey "guys" who worked in the Harvey House kitchens, I was impressed by their pride in work well done and their sincere interest in helping others. The history of the Fred Harvey

Union Station, Paris, Texas.—3

The Paris, Texas Santa Fe Depot contained a Fred Harvey Newsstand. The restored depot now houses the Paris Economic Development Corporation and the research library of the Lamar County Genealogical Society. *Courtesy of Michael McMillan.*

Exterior of the restored railroad depot and Harvey House in Brownwood, Texas. *Author's collection.*

business is interesting as well. It all began in 1876 with a handshake agreement between Mr. Harvey and the Santa Fe Railroad. Because of Harvey's keen business sense and commitment to high standards, the company continued to thrive even after his death twenty-five years later when his two sons, Ford and Byron, took over leadership. At that time, the decision was made to call the company "Fred Harvey." As you read this book, you will note references to Fred Harvey and the Fred Harvey company. Although I use these interchangeably, references to either after Mr. Harvey's death in 1901 are referring to the company, not the individual.

There is an interesting diversity in the nature of each Texas Harvey House and the manner in which the structures were or were not preserved. For example, the Harvey House in Slaton has been renovated and now operates as a bed-and-breakfast. In Sweetwater, where four railroad lines converged, all that remains of the Harvey House is a partial concrete slab. And so it was with the history of individuals who worked for Fred Harvey, some for a year or less, others for decades. While searching for personal stories of Harvey employees, especially Harvey Girls, I placed notices in Texas newspapers asking for information, and I traveled to most of the Texas Harvey House locations searching for photographs and family stories. I was genuinely thrilled when a connection was made and someone shared a personal memory or letter. Unfortunately, the resources were not evenly distributed, leaving me with an abundance of information relating to most of the Texas Harvey Houses but with little history for others. This is, in part, due to the lack of structured employee records during Harvey House years and, in part, because personal mementos, letters and photos were lost during the passage of time.

Almost twenty years ago, Arizona artist Tina Mion and her husband, Allan Affeldt, purchased and restored the last Fred Harvey hotel, La Posada, in Winslow, Arizona. (It is beautiful! Recently, the couple began the process to purchase and restore another Harvey hotel, Castaneda, in Las Vegas, New Mexico.) When the couple moved to Winslow, they became close friends with former Harvey Girls who still lived in the area. Mion produced a painting titled *The Last Harvey Girl* depicting two of these long-retired women: Ruby McHood and Dorothy Hunt. In the painting, Ruby is wearing a white blouse, a black bow tie and a skirt adorned with colorful applique and trim. This Harvey Girl uniform was typically worn in tourist-savvy Harvey Houses in New Mexico, Arizona and California. As Dorothy sits in the shadows, hands folded in her lap, Ruby stands, leaning on a walking cane, holding a cup of tea. She appears to be offering the tea to the viewer.

Texas Harvey House locations. *Map by Melissa Morrow.*

In a statement about the painting, the artist said, "Only a handful of Harvey Girls remain. One day soon, someone will be handed a cup of tea or coffee by the last Harvey Girl and, in an anonymous kitchen or living room, an era will silently pass." The artist intends for the viewer to be the honored recipient of the passing of this era.

The Harvey Girl era has indeed slipped away. This book is a celebration of the experiences and accomplishments of these hardworking, adventuresome women and a reminder of how Fred Harvey and his Harvey Girls changed the culture of Texas railroad towns along the Atchison, Topeka and Santa Fe. I am grateful for the opportunity to share their story.

Chapter 1
LAYING TRACKS FOR TEXAS CULTURE

THE FRED HARVEY STORY

When Fred Harvey pushed his chain of restaurants farther and farther west along the lengthening tracks of the Santa Fe, he brought with him one of the first civilizing forces this land had known: the Harvey Girls. These winsome waitresses conquered the West as surely as David Crockett and the Kit Carsons—not with powder horn and rifle but with a beefsteak and a cup of coffee.
—Introduction to the 1946 MGM movie The Harvey Girls

In the late nineteenth century, as the Santa Fe Railroad stretched down through Texas and continued west to California, the railroad company began to work diligently to develop passenger travel to help pay for the expansion. This was not an easy task. Train travel was not comfortable. Passenger cars provided minimal shelter as they traveled through weather extremes from chilly, snow-capped mountains to windblown, summer-scorched prairies. Smoke, soot and dirt filled the air, choking even the hardiest of travelers.

Having food available during a long train trip was especially difficult. Nothing was offered on board. Some passengers brought their own baskets of food and hoped they would last through the entire trip. Overpriced beans and stale biscuits might be available at a saloon during a remote fuel stop; however, this food of questionable quality was often inedible.

With years of experience as a railroad agent, solicitor and mail clerk, Fred Harvey knew firsthand how difficult it was to get decent food while traveling by

Fred Harvey, founder of Harvey House restaurants, newsstands and hotels. Harvey is credited for bringing a high standard of hospitality to towns along the Santa Fe Railroad. *Courtesy of kansasmemory.org, Kansas State Historical Society.*

train, and because of previous restaurant experience, he believed he had a solution to the problem. Harvey's first job after immigrating to the United States from England had been as a pot scrubber and busboy in a New York restaurant. Later, he owned a café in St. Louis, Missouri, that catered to wealthy businessmen who expected fast service and good food served in tasteful surroundings.

Fred Harvey knew how to run a successful restaurant in the city, and he believed he could duplicate the same quality for railroad passengers along the line. When Harvey met with Santa Fe officials in 1876, he told them he was confident he could personally change the miserable reputation of railway dining into something train passengers would actually look forward to eating. With a handshake, the gentlemen agreed to make Harvey Houses a reality, and the first restaurant chain in the United States began.

As Fred Harvey grew his chain of trackside restaurants, when a location was deemed appropriate for a Harvey establishment, the Santa Fe would design and build space in the new depot building for the kitchen, food storage, a lunch counter and, in some places, a dining room, as well as living quarters for Harvey employees. This space, built especially for Fred Harvey's business venture, was called a Harvey House. But Mr. Harvey didn't need newly built, elegant surroundings to maintain his standard of service with linens, china and silver. In one of his first Harvey House locations in Holbrook, Arizona, he set up in five boxcars close to the railroad tracks. The exteriors were "painted red and decorated with large geometric Indian designs. The atmosphere inside was of subdued elegance. Tables were set with Irish linen, Sheffield silver and china from France; fresh cut flowers from California stood beside great pitchers of ice water." The menu featured exotic fare such as terrapin, antelope, quail and oysters as well as beefsteak. Patrons could choose from several different wines. Harvey would have nothing but the best service for such an elegant meal, and only the Harvey Girls could meet his standard.

How *did* the idea of Harvey Girls come about? It seems it all began in the tiny, remote northern New Mexico town of Raton in the late 1880s when a Harvey House was established. An all-male staff served the eating house patrons, consisting mostly of miners, cowboys and railroad men. Following an after-hours fight involving the staff, no one was able to work the next morning. When word of the situation reached Fred Harvey, he took the train to Raton to remedy the situation. An enraged Harvey fired everyone and hired a new manager, Tom Gable. Gable proposed replacing the disorderly men with attractive young women, correctly reasoning that the women would be more reliable and cause less trouble. He believed the change in staff would also be well received by train passengers and the community. Harvey agreed. Using popular women's magazines and newspapers, he began advertising for "attractive and intelligent young women 18 to 20 years of age" to move to the West for employment.

The young women who answered Fred Harvey's call did so for different reasons. Some were simply looking for a way to leave the family farm and explore the possibilities for a different lifestyle. Others realized the money they could make as a Harvey Girl would pay for the education needed for a career in teaching or nursing. A portion of the applicants were simply looking for adventure. Surely all of the Harvey Girl hopefuls were keenly aware that working in a remote place where few women lived would provide many opportunities for meeting a prospective husband. If somehow this possibility escaped a young woman, newspaper and magazine articles often emphasized certain benefits with phrases such as: "Sensible girls got their men by going where the men were."

Harvey Girls personalized the Fred Harvey standards and brought their eastern and midwestern sensibilities to a job that previously had not been held in high esteem. Harvey's strict rules about dressing modestly, wearing little or no makeup and conducting oneself in a respectable manner served the purpose of reassuring the young ladies that they would be in good company, working and living with like-minded women. Their reputations would be protected even far from home where they would be judged without benefit of a family's good reputation.

At the time early Harvey Girls were hired, workingwomen were not typically held in high esteem unless they were teachers or nurses. Waitressing, in particular, was considered one of the lowest professions a woman could choose and was certainly not a proper profession for a white, middle-class young woman. In the West, many waitresses were also prostitutes, and even when this was not true, the perception prevailed. Usually, tough, coarse women were the only ones who could make it alone in remote, rural areas. The sheltered living circumstances provided for Harvey Girls made it possible for more refined women to survive in uncivilized, developing railroad towns.

Fred Harvey's rules were a dominant part of any Harvey Girl's experience, but they served many a good purpose. In addition to providing a protective aura for the women, the rules standardized service in Harvey Houses and helped sell the Harvey ideal all along the Santa Fe. Just as Fred Harvey changed the standards for food and service for train passengers, he changed the standards for the job of a waitress. Harvey Girls were expected to conduct themselves in a ladylike manner at all times. This conduct changed the public perception of working, single women, especially waitresses.

The ambitious, venturesome young women who passed the rigorous personal interview at the Kansas City, Missouri or Chicago, Illinois Harvey offices were given a train pass to their new jobs and often left immediately. The company only accepted women who were educated, neatly dressed and groomed and who spoke clearly and showed good manners. At this point in the development of Fred Harvey's chain of restaurants, all Harvey Girls were single and were required to sign a contract stipulating they would not marry during the first six months of employment. Between 1883 and the late 1950s, approximately 100,000 Harvey Girls proudly wore the now famous black-and-white uniforms.

Fred Harvey's rules for his employees, especially Harvey Girls, are legendary. This set of rules posted in employee living quarters is dated 1887:

> *Employees are requested not to scratch matches, drive nails or tacks, or any other way mar the walls of their rooms.*
> *No rubbish of any kind must be thrown in the toilets.*
> *Bath tubs* [sic] *must be thoroughly cleaned by employes* [sic] *after using.*
> *Loud talking and laughing in rooms and halls should be avoided.*
> *Employes* [sic] *must be in their rooms by 11:00 o'clock p.m. unless given special permission by manager to remain out longer.*
> *Rooms must be kept in tidy condition and wearing apparel must be kept in its proper place.*
> *Expectorating on floors is positively forbidden.*
> *The purpose of the above rules is to bring about a tidy and homelike*

condition in your rooms and we request your co-operation so that the desired results will be brought about.

Fred Harvey

Consistent food quality was valued as much as quality of service. According to a story in *Santa Fe Magazine* in 1907, the manager of each Harvey House was required to send a tabulated report at the end of each day. The purpose of the reports was not to assess possible ways of reducing expenses but to ensure that the Harvey standard was maintained: "that the slices of ham in the Harvey sandwiches are as thick as ever and the same thickness everywhere and that the coffee is as strong as it should be." In Harvey Houses, whole pies were cut into four servings instead of the usual six or eight in other restaurants. The daily reports reflected the inventory of food used in relation to the number of customers served, indicating that portions were up to Harvey standards. Many Harvey Houses operated in the red for years. Fred Harvey's business philosophy was simple. He believed that profits would come in the long run if excellent service was provided and maintained.

After struggling with cancer for more than fifteen years, Fred Harvey died in 1901 at the age of sixty-five. That year, he owned and operated fifteen hotels, forty-seven restaurants, thirty dining cars and a San Francisco Bay ferry. The eulogy delivered at his funeral was a tribute to his life; however, now we know that it was also an apt description of what the name "Fred Harvey" would mean for many years to come: "Fred Harvey is dead, but his spirit still lives. The standard of excellence he set can never go back. He has been a civilizer and benefactor. He has added to the physical, mental, and spiritual welfare of millions. Fred Harvey simply kept faith with the public. He gave pretty nearly a perfect service."

Following Fred Harvey's death, his sons, Ford and Byron, continued to operate the substantial family business. The decision was made for the company name to be simply "Fred Harvey," maintaining the illusion that the founder was still alive. For years after Mr. Harvey's death, employees continued to say they worked for Fred Harvey; in correspondence and printed marketing pieces, the company was referred to as "Fred Harvey." There was some speculation that Ford Harvey, who was appointed president of the company after his father's death, may have chosen this company name because of a lack of self-confidence. However, with his movie-star good looks and experience of working beside his father for many years, I'm inclined to believe Ford realized this would be a smart marketing tactic. And it was!

Ahead of its time, the Fred Harvey company was establishing its brand over a century before "branding" became a buzzword. The Fred Harvey logo, composed simply of Mr. Harvey's signature, was attached to high-quality products such as coffee, whiskey and cigars. Fred Harvey fruit preserves were served at breakfast. For a time, Coca-Cola bottles produced in Newton, Kansas, had the imprint "Fred Harvey Newton" on the bottom. Harvey Houses are credited with originating the "blue-plate special," a daily low-priced complete meal that was served on a blue-patterned china plate. An 1892 Harvey menu mentions this dining option some thirty years before it became a common restaurant term. In the United States until the early 1960s when the country's eating habits began to change, ordering the blue-plate or daily special in a café or diner meant you got a meal predetermined by the restaurant usually consisting of meat, vegetables and bread served on one plate for a reduced price.

Whenever possible, the Fred Harvey company encouraged publicity about its food and hotel service with the use of well-placed newspaper and magazine articles. An often-used phrase was that Fred Harvey set the desert abloom with beefsteaks. A 1940s article printed in the *American Mercury* magazine and reprinted in *Reader's Digest* cleverly described Fred Harvey as "turning a shoestring potato into a 2,500-mile string of railroad eating places." The article also said that Harvey "unconsciously launched a 'matrimonial bureau' which played a major role in civilizing the Southwest." The article posed the question, "How did these romances pan out? All along the route of the Santa Fe you can talk with fine young college men and girls proud that Mother once worked for Fred Harvey and met Dad over the pie counter. Almost every substantial family in the Southwest boasts a Harvey Girl in the family somewhere."

HARVEY GIRLS ON THE SILVER SCREEN

One extremely clever marketing tactic was an agreement between Fred Harvey and Metro Goldwyn Mayer to make a movie about Harvey Girls. Described by one critic as a glorified commercial for the Fred Harvey restaurants, the 1946 MGM movie *The Harvey Girls* may have done the most for perpetuating the story of the Harvey waitresses. The movie featured celebrities of the time—Judy Garland, Ray Bolger and Angela Lansbury—and can still be seen occasionally on the Turner Classic Movie channel. The song "On the Atchison,

Promotional postcard for the 1946 movie *The Harvey Girls*, featuring Judy Garland. *Courtesy of Michael McMillan.*

Topeka and the Santa Fe," sung by Garland, won an Academy Award for songwriter Johnnie Mercer.

According to correspondence with Metro Goldwyn Mayer Pictures, Fred Harvey executives exerted great influence on the advertising of the movie as well as the movie itself. In a move to appease the Harvey family, Byron Harvey Jr., grandson of Fred Harvey, was given a cameo as a Santa Fe railroad brakeman.

An October 1945 telegram from Byron Harvey Sr., Fred Harvey's son and president of the company, to the MGM publicity department complained that the magazine and billboard advertising gave "the erroneous impression that this picture is largely a burlesque show or that the Harvey Girls were dance hall girls. In my opinion this type of advertising not only misrepresents the general character of the picture but is highly damaging to our company and its employees and is directly contrary to the spirit of our understanding." Byron referred to a letter written to MGM the previous year when he specified "that the production should be of such high quality that any publicity which the Fred Harvey system may derive from the picture will be of a favorable nature." Byron indicated that even though he had not seen the Harvey Girl movie, a Harvey company representative had told him that "the studio has sincerely tried to carry out our mutual understanding. However, I feel very strongly that any favorable publicity our company and its employees may derive from the picture itself will be more than offset by such sensational advertising as is now apparently being produced."

The following day, from his New York office, Howard Dietz, chief publicist and director of advertising for MGM, responded to the midwestern executive in a somewhat condescending tone, saying, "I have gone over the ads and while we do use the dancing girl motif quite frequently it does not seem to be used offensively and is consistent with the idea of a musical picture." Dietz promised that "wherever possible in material not yet prepared we shall do our best to tone down what you consider objectionable and also attempt to make it clear that the Harvey Girls were not burlesque queens." With a conciliatory note, Dietz concluded, "I shall be extremely uncomfortable if you are dissatisfied with the treatment of the film and I want to do everything I can to find a common ground."

Telegrams continued between the two powerful men, with Byron stating the he found it "particularly objectionable" that Dietz's posters prominently featured "Alhambra [the saloon in the movie] girls with only minor picturization of Harvey Girls and with the wording 'The Harvey Girls' appearing opposite Angela Lansbury's legs." Harvey goes on to call the MGM advertising plan an "exploitation manual" and criticizes proposed slogans for newspaper advertising. "If these slogans reflect your people's conception of the Harvey Girls picture I cannot help but feel deeply regretful for having given permission for this production. I hope you can send one of your responsible assistants to show me other proposed advertising and to explain what steps are being taken to overcome my objections."

Byron Harvey also declined an invitation to come to New York for a screening of the movie and stated, "I do hope you will decide to arrange a private showing for me in Chicago at an early date, as previously promised by your people in New York and Hollywood."

The Fred Harvey company might have had a difficult time bringing New York and Hollywood up to its standards, but the Harvey home office continued to maintain strict control over its establishments. Exacting details were sent to Harvey managers concerning advertising and promotion of the Harvey Girl movie. Small posters were sent to all locations, and managers were told to attach them "on the bulletin board in the kitchen or fastened with gummed tape to the wall in a prominent location" so waitresses and "your entire crew" would see them. The coordinated, promotional message to the Harvey employees was: "Millions are seeing *The Harvey Girls* on the screen and many of them will see us every day. Let's all be at our best!"

Freestanding cutouts of Judy Garland in her Harvey Girl movie costume were also provided to promote the upcoming movie. Managers were instructed to not only acknowledge to the Fred Harvey main office that they received the cardboard figures, but they were also to send an exact description of where they were going to be displayed. Large "Judy" displays were sent to Harvey Houses in El Paso and Houston; Temple, Fort Worth and Amarillo received smaller versions; and Brownwood and Galveston locations received a large and a small display.

Another example of the advertising acumen of the Fred Harvey company were special menus featuring promotional photos. These were distributed in December 1945 with instructions not to use them too far in advance of the premiere of the movie planned for January 1946. During this same time, Fred Harvey ran magazine advertising captioned, "What…a movie about us?" Byron Harvey included this reminder in a letter to managers, "In order for us to reap the potential benefits from this motion picture, it is necessary for us to have our house in order—standards of service, food, cleanliness, courtesy, and personnel at the very highest peak. We realize all this comes to us at a time when we are still very busy with the many problems left over from the war. Nevertheless we should grasp this opportunity and make the most of it. I am counting on all of you to do your very best to this end." The Fred Harvey company was doing business, forty years later, in the same way that Fred Harvey, the man, had done before his death. And as originally intended, the attention to detail and service was a major windfall to tourism in the southwestern and western United States as thousands traveled by rail knowing that Fred Harvey would take care of them.

The very first Harvey House opened in 1876 in Topeka, Kansas, and the first Texas Harvey House opened in 1897 in Galveston. The last Harvey establishment to open in Texas was Brownwood in 1914, thirteen years after the death of Fred Harvey.

Across the United States after World War II, automobiles became more affordable, and passenger train travel declined. Ironically, the Fred Harvey company became its own strongest competitor when "Meals by Fred Harvey" were introduced on railroad dining cars. With high-quality food and beverages available on the train, there was no reason for passengers to eat at the Harvey House. Additionally, diesel fuel replaced steam, and frequent fuel stops were no longer necessary.

As times changed, the Fred Harvey restaurant system had to move to where most passengers went—airports and resorts. In 1968, the company supervised food service on the dining cars of the Santa Fe Railway in an operation that extended over thirteen thousand miles of railroad track. By this time, many Harvey locations had closed, but railroad stations such as Chicago's Union Station remained important because of a concentration of commuter traffic. A company report stated that approximately a dozen Harvey restaurants and gift shops were still operating at that time.

The Fred Harvey company became a subsidiary of Amfac, Inc. in 1968. Through a merger in the early 1990s, all that remained of the Fred Harvey company—El Tovar and Bright Angel Lodge at the Grand Canyon—became part of Xanterra, the largest parks concession management company in the United States. On its website, www.xanterra.com, the company refers to the Fred Harvey company's proven expertise and Xanterra's commitment to those principles in today's hospitality business.

Chapter 2

ALWAYS FRESH EGGS

RURAL TEXAS HARVEY HOUSES

The aroma most enticing,
Blending with the steam,
The face across the hazy cup.
The vision of a queen.

I like my morning coffee,
Before the busy noon,
When she has time to chatter,
While I dally with my spoon.

All dressed in spotless linen,
Her hair all in a curl,
So purely sweetly winning,
Is the happy Harvey Girl.
—*John Moore,* Amarillo Globe, *1931*

During the earlier years when Harvey Houses were established in remote locations, it was necessary to recruit women who were willing to move great distances for a job. By the time the trackside restaurants began to open in Texas, there was a fairly large network of experienced Harvey Girls available to bring the Harvey way to new locations, and most of the towns in Texas were already somewhat "civilized." At the time the Brownwood Harvey House opened in 1914, there were two coed colleges in the town. Many of the intelligent women of good character who worked in Texas Harvey Houses were local women or from other Texas towns within the region. Rather than traveling to the Kansas City Fred Harvey office for a personal interview, most were hired on recommendation from a local citizen or the Harvey staff. Those women who did move to Texas to take a job in a Harvey House often stayed and made the adopted state their home. The influence of Harvey Girls on the Texas towns where they worked has been passed down through generations.

An efficient, somewhat mysterious "cup code" helped streamline the service to harried train passengers. After diners were seated, a waitress would ask whether they preferred coffee, tea, iced tea or milk. She would then arrange the cup at the place setting before each patron and move to the next table. Soon the "drink girl" would arrive at the table and magically pour the patron's preferred drink without asking. If the waitress left the cup right side up in its saucer, that meant coffee; upside down meant hot tea; upside down but tilted against the saucer meant iced tea; and upside down, away from the saucer meant milk.

The Harvey Girls were essential for successful Harvey House operations, working closely with other staff to provide delicious food and quick, efficient service. Salad and sandwich boys, ice cream boys and bakers or pastry boys worked long hours alongside the chef to prepare food consistent with the Harvey standards. Many former Harvey employees described the work environment as being like a family.

As new Harvey Houses opened in Texas, it was not uncommon for experienced chefs, originally from Europe, to transfer from Harvey restaurants in other states. The immigrant chefs were generally described as temperamental men whose stormy personalities often clashed with the resolute Harvey Girls.

The Harvey House manager played a key role in the lives of all the staff, but especially that of the Harvey Girls. The Harvey standards were always upheld; however, the manager and his wife were usually remembered as displaying kindness and understanding in helping young women who were often away from home for the first time.

The policy forbidding Harvey Girls to date Harvey staff or Santa Fe employees, usually referred to as "railroad men," appeared to be somewhat relaxed in Texas. Occasionally, married couples were both hired, and it wasn't unusual for the manager of a Texas Harvey House to employ a married woman. However, there were plenty of single women who lived on the premises under the watchful eyes of the manager's wife, and many a Harvey Girl circumvented the curfew with the help of sympathetic kitchen helpers.

Although Harvey Girls earned up to thirty-five dollars a month, very good wages for the time, long hours on the job usually precluded shopping sprees. In some Texas towns, there were few opportunities for socializing. When asked about keeping curfew, one young woman indicated it wasn't difficult to abide by the rules since "there was nothing to do to anyway, just time to rest and read."

Numerous previous Harvey staff came out of retirement to help feed American soldiers and foreign prisoners of war transported by train across the United States during World War II. This was a difficult experience for the former Harvey employees. The work was exhausting, and the ideals set forth by Fred Harvey many years before were sacrificed to meet the demands of serving and preparing hundreds of meals daily. Linen tablecloths were abandoned; however, linen napkins were still used. Meals were no longer cooked to order, instead food was prepared in large quantities and kept warm throughout the day. Many of the menu items offered when Harvey Houses were thriving were unavailable during wartime due to food rationing.

During this same time, Fred Harvey was using magazine advertising to put a positive spin on changes that occurred while the company was serving the troop trains. One ad shows a drawing of an older woman with a picture of a Harvey Girl in the background. The headline, "Back in the ranks…" leads into copy, "and she's always on call to help in a pinch at Fred Harvey's—the same Harvey House where she was a Harvey Girl forty years ago. Except for patriotic women like her, many of our young fighting men would go hungry." The ad further explains that "to do this job and do it well—in spite of help shortages, rationing and our greatly increased civilian patronage—is now our foremost task. If this occasionally means we cannot give you the old-time Fred Harvey service, we know you understand. When our war job is done we promise you only Harvey hospitality at its very best."

In reality, the thousands of troops traveling by train added greatly to the Harvey House customer base at a time when civilian train travel was waning, bringing profits back to some sites that had been closed for several years. The results of a smart, extensive marketing effort coupled with the enduring Harvey reputation and an increase in patrons were very positive for the company. According to inter-company memos, Fred Harvey served over forty-one million meals and brought in a gross income of over $37 million in 1945, the largest in the company's seventy-year history.

A great, eloquent fan of the Santa Fe and Fred Harvey, Elbert Hubbard wrote the following review of the two companies in 1909: "The railroad company builds for the future. These men, with prophetic vision, know that the traffic will eventually warrant the expenditure, even if it does not now.

They set their stakes and the world comes to them. Thus does the Octopus [the railroad] do for civilization what your detached and individual citizens can never do for themselves." And using Mr. Hubbard's analogy, indeed the successful "octopus" that was the Fred Harvey company began to spread across the great state of Texas.

CLEBURNE (1899–1931)

In the red brick two-story depot building constructed in 1894, Fred Harvey operated a lunchroom and newsstand in Cleburne from 1899 until 1931. As was the norm for a Harvey House restaurant, the Cleburne Lunch Room was known for having the finest food in town. The large kitchen was downstairs, and customers were served at a horseshoe-shaped bar; there was no dining room. The Harvey House manager and Harvey Girls had apartments upstairs.

Raymond Nichols began work as a pantry boy in 1923 at this Harvey House location. He recalled the experience in a letter to the author: "I got the job through a neighbor who worked as Head Waitress. I worked this position for several months, 6 a.m. to 6 p.m. until I was promoted to night waiter, 6 p.m. to 6 a.m. I was paid one dollar per day and furnished room and board by Fred Harvey." However, by moving to the night shift, Nichols was able to attend Mrs. Cullen's School of Business, where, among other things, he learned shorthand and typing. In 1926, after finishing school, he was offered a position as secretary to the Santa Fe superintendent for the Northern Division. In this position, Nichols earned $165 a month, "but I had to furnish my own room and board."

Just as it was with some Harvey Girls, Harvey guys used their experience and training to build careers beyond working for Fred Harvey. Nichols opened his own restaurant in 1945. "Because of my experience with Fred Harvey, which was an A-1 operation in every respect, I decided I was qualified to own and operate a restaurant on my own. Working in the Harvey House gave me the courage to start my own business." Nichols's first restaurant was very successful, and he began building drive-in restaurants, including the famous Lone Star Drive In Restaurants in Fort Worth and Dallas. Raymond stated, "From my thirty dollar per month job with Fred Harvey I became a millionaire by 1960. My point in mentioning my progress through life is so you will understand my very warm feeling and appreciation for being hired

Railroad depots and Harvey House in Cleburne, Texas. *Courtesy of Michael McMillan.*

Harvey House chefs and kitchen staff displaying various tools of their trade in Cleburne, Texas. *Courtesy of Layland Museum, Cleburne, Texas.*

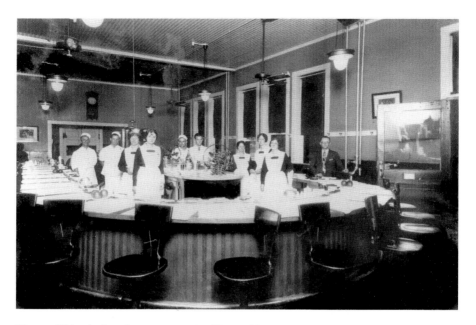

Harvey Girls, chefs and managers at the Harvey House Lunch Room in Cleburne, Texas. *Courtesy of Layland Museum, Cleburne, Texas.*

at eight cents per hour. Needless to say the name Fred Harvey still brings good thoughts to my mind."

Fresh baked breads and homemade pies were a hit with Cleburne Harvey House customers. These were provided for quite some time by baker Zip Plemons. Lola Lassitter, a Cleburne Harvey Girl during the early 1920s, remembered the baker "as a little ol' guy. He wasn't any bigger than a bar of soap. He could really get around. He'd come in with a tray of pies like you never saw. He also made cookies and angel food cakes—the prettiest you ever saw."

Lola, who was known as "Hootus," also recalled working early in the morning, often starting as early as 4:00 a.m. The pantry boy, Shorty, would wake the women up for this pre-dawn shift. "Shorty had the oranges sliced and peeled and everything ready when we'd come downstairs. The pay was good. We lived there and slept there and did everything except our wash." Lola also remembered that most of the railroad men wanted steaks later in the day; however, "if it was morning they'd all come in and flop down at the counter and say, 'Bring me a bowl of mush!' That was oatmeal." There was the ever-present, large, shiny Harvey House coffee urn, and milk was kept in a pitcher set in ice inside a low counter. Fresh fruits and vegetables were characteristic of a good Harvey House meal, and patrons were served only fresh eggs, usually purchased daily from local farmers.

Many Harvey Girls recalled the requirement to wear a hair net when serving customers; however, the management of the Cleburne Harvey House took this one step further. Jewell Curtis began working at this location in 1918. However, her Harvey Girl career ended seven years later when she succumbed to the new flapper hairstyles and was fired for cutting her hair.

Charles Everett Wilson came to Cleburne in the summer of 1904 from the Newburg, Missouri Harvey House to work as a cook. Wilson had previously worked for the Santa Fe Railroad, but after an injury, he trained to be a cook, a skill that was to be his lifelong profession. In 1905, Wilson was offered a job as an apprentice to a French chef at the Grand Canyon in Arizona, where Fred Harvey was building the El Tovar Hotel and Restaurant. He chose not accept that position and moved to Sherman, Texas, instead to work for the Binkley Hotel. In a letter I received from Mr. Wilson's daughter, Ruth Wilson Strawn, relating his Harvey House career, she stated that she believes that her dad always regretted that decision.

Cleburne Harvey Girls, as in the majority of Harvey Houses, were forbidden to mix with the railroad men or other customers. However, in a small rural town, what was a girl to do? In Cleburne, there may have been more railroad men to choose from than other locations. At one time, it was headquarters for one of the largest repair facilities on the Santa Fe line between Galveston and Chicago. In 1904, over 1,400 Cleburne residents were employed by the railroad. According to a report in the *Cleburne Eagle News*, at its peak, more than five hundred engines and six thousand boxcars were repaired at the Santa Fe facility each year. "Its infrastructure, comprising 232 acres and 67 miles of track, had its own fire department, telephone system and water supply."

The former Cleburne Santa Fe shops were torn down during the 1990s to clear a way for road improvements. The depot building, where the Harvey House once proudly served the community and train passengers, no longer exists.

ROSENBERG (1899–1923)

At the time the Harvey House was built in Rosenberg, the population of the town was less than eight hundred. As early as the 1830s, the city was a small

shipping point on the Brazos River. In 1883, the Gulf, Colorado and Santa Fe Railway purchased the site, two hundred acres in all, and platted a town. The two-story Union Station was built the same year, and a Harvey House opened next door in 1899. Both the depot and Harvey House were frame structures on blocks two to three feet above street level. An elevated plank boardwalk, lined with banana trees and other foliage, joined the two buildings.

A prominent sign, "Lunch Room Fred Harvey," drew train passengers to the Harvey House. Those who took a meal at this restaurant were greeted with a polished lunch counter surrounded by high-backed, swivel wooden stools, as well as dining tables with all of the Harvey finery. Hurricane lantern–style lamps hung from a wooden-beamed ceiling. Inside the restaurant was a Harvey Newsstand where magazines and other periodicals, as well as an assortment of cigars, were sold. This Harvey restaurant was smaller than many others along the Santa Fe in Texas; however, Harvey standards were maintained, and the staff was dedicated and well trained. In 1909, manager P.N. Loso was transferred from Rosenberg to lend his expertise to the opening of the new Harvey House in Vaughn, New Mexico.

Harvey Girls have the reputation of having civilized the rural towns where they worked through their contributions to church and community activities. Often, a new Harvey Girl would come from poor rural circumstances, yet she would introduce a love for reading or artistic talent to her adopted home. Many farm girls who became part of the Harvey family were thrust into a

Above: Harvey House Lunch Room in Rosenberg, Texas. *Courtesy of Fort Bend County Museum Association, Richmond, Texas.*

Left: Three Harvey Girls on the boardwalk between the Harvey House and the depot in Rosenberg, Texas. *Courtesy of Fort Bend County Museum Association, Richmond, Texas.*

Opposite: Railroad depot and Harvey House in Rosenberg, Texas. *Courtesy of Fort Bend County Museum Association, Richmond, Texas.*

world where, for perhaps the first time, they were encouraged to be feminine and take pride in their appearance. The transition was easy to accomplish in the clean surroundings of the Harvey Girl living arrangement with plenty of hot water, some privacy and a dresser with a mirror.

Other Harvey employees also contributed to the culture in the towns where they worked. In Rosenberg, the wife of one Harvey House manager, Hazel Studley, taught piano lessons. In addition, typically the manager's wife was given the responsibility of chaperoning the Harvey Girls and undoubtedly influenced the young girls. Dating a Harvey employee or railroad man was forbidden, but certain managers relaxed the rule, allowing couples to see one another in the public area of the girls' living space or on the front porch. Occasionally, a walk to the Santa Fe Reading Room or the park or attending Wednesday night prayer meeting together might be permitted. Once a couple began attending Sunday morning services together, everyone knew a wedding would soon follow.

Harvey company records show that the Rosenberg Harvey House ceased operations in 1923. Some reports say the depot and Harvey House burned that year, but that is unconfirmed. Neither the depot nor the Harvey building can be seen in photographs of the area taken in 1924, but exactly what happened to the Rosenberg Harvey House is still somewhat of a mystery.

TEMPLE (1899–1933)

Beginning in 1899, the Fred Harvey company operated a lunchroom, dining room, newsstand and trackside hotel in Temple and a dairy and farm just outside of town. Twelve years later, almost $2,000 was appropriated to fund improvements to the park adjoining the Temple hotel. The park was doubled in size, and fountains and cement walks were installed, providing an attractive landscape for a new passenger station and three-story, fireproof hotel. The original frame hotel was moved to a new location and converted to a laundry for service to Harvey Houses in Texas.

The hotel was for both travelers and Santa Fe employees. When Laura Worsham and her husband, Sidney, chief dispatcher for the Santa Fe Railroad, came to Temple, they lived in the Harvey Hotel until they found a home. The Temple Harvey House was the nicest eating establishment at the time and often the site of special club meetings, school dances and dinners.

Santa Fe Train Station and Harvey House in Temple, Texas. *Courtesy of Michael McMillan.*

Harvey House Dining Room in Temple, Texas. *Courtesy of ATSFry.com, R.L. Crump Library Collection, Copy and Reuse Restrictions Apply.*

J.E. Bobo was a manager in the Harvey system and was mentioned in several Harvey Girl interviews. He worked at the Temple Harvey House in 1924 and 1925. He was also cashier at the Somerville Harvey House (1928) and manager of the Canadian Harvey House (1934–36) and the Brownwood Harvey House (1945–46). In a monthly magazine for Santa Fe Railroad and Harvey House employees, it was noted that Temple chef Frank Allen had worked for the Harvey system for sixteen years, and baker Frank Reusch was a Harvey employee for twelve years.

The Temple Harvey Hotel manager for ten years beginning in 1906, P.A. Craig, was featured in *Santa Fe Magazine*. The story stated: "In addition to the fine management of the Harvey Hotel, P.A. also oversaw one of the finest dairies in the South." The 275-acre dairy supplied milk and cream to all Harvey Houses in the Texas Division of the Harvey system. With the help of the dairy foreman, Mr. Craig entered an exhibit that year in the Bell County Fair that was touted as one of the principal attractions in central Texas during the fall season. According to printed reports, the exhibit was considered one of the prettiest, most interesting and educational exhibits that Temple had seen in years. "The best milk cows were there—one whose daily average is nine gallons, or seventy-two pounds of milk—each cow being groomed to perfection and covered with a beautiful Santa Fe–Fred Harvey blue and white blanket." Harvey Girls, dressed as Swiss milk maids, led the cows, and the "finest chickens on the farm were displayed, as were the finest turkeys, and, to lend dignity to the procession, the finest bull was marched along." The news story also mentions a poultry float and a "large white Holland turkey with ribbon streamers." No doubt, the Harvey folks put on quite a show!

During the time Erna Koen was a Temple Harvey Girl (1926–28), she began to notice—and be noticed by—Lester Johnson, who worked at the Harvey Dairy. He had transferred to Temple as a milkman from the Fred Harvey Dairy in Kansas City. "We didn't hold the pies to the next day," Erna explained. "If there were any left after we had served all the trains for the day, we were supposed to throw them out." However, at the end of the day, if there was a pie left, Erna would leave it outside the back door of the Harvey House. She knew Lester would be delighted to find the treat when he made his early delivery of dairy products the next day. "We became friends and were married." A year later, Erna and Lester started their own dairy farm.

Lena Warren Gericke worked at the Temple Harvey House in 1924–25, but because she was only seventeen years old when hired, she could work only in the kitchen the first year, as Harvey Girls had to be at least eighteen years

Harvey House Lunch Room in Temple, Texas. *Courtesy of ATSFry.com, R.L. Crump Library Collection, Copy and Reuse Restrictions Apply.*

Scenic Santa Fe Park, depot and Harvey House in Temple, Texas. *Courtesy of Michael McMillan.*

old. She was paid thirty dollars a month with room and board; uniforms and laundry were furnished.

Etta Lanham Williams saw employment as a Harvey Girl as a chance to get away from home. Her mother died when Etta was thirteen, and she was the only girl on a farm near Holland, Texas, with four brothers. When describing life on the farm, Etta said, "Those brothers were more strict than Harvey rules!" A relative in Temple heard about jobs at the Harvey House and encouraged her to apply. While working in Temple from 1920 until 1924, Etta was sent to the Harvey House in Brownwood, Texas, for special training, after which she was put in charge of the banquet facilities. "The banquets were very well appointed. Fancy! And it was really something to go to a banquet at the Harvey House." Looking back at her Harvey Girl years, Etta recalled, "The attitude of the public toward a young woman who needed to work was different back then. We worked long hours, seven days a week most of the time. There were no benefits such as unemployment insurance, health insurance or retirement plans." There were other benefits, though, as Etta believed that her Harvey House experience helped her develop socially and taught her about the nice things in life. After leaving her job to marry a railroad man, Etta was very active in the Eastern Star organization, was past president of the Churchwomen of Temple and Bell County and played the piano and taught Sunday school for fifty years at Memorial Baptist Church in Temple.

According to a story in the *Temple Daily Telegram* in the 1920s, "Nothing has been spared to make the Temple Harvey House one of the most attractive houses on the line." The local newspaper also told about "Santa Fe engineer Col. Avery Parson who recently was a passenger on the Temple Northwestern Special" who, "regardless of the fact that an enormous supply of edibles had been placed on board," also got a Harvey House lunch to take with him. The colonel said that a "railroad man couldn't get out without getting something from Harvey." An unnamed Harvey executive added, "It is a good habit to patronize the Harvey people. The majority of our girls measure up to the high standard of their environment and are keenly alive to their opportunities of self-advancement."

The Temple Harvey House building has been demolished; however, the adjacent 1911 Prairie-style depot has been restored and houses the Santa Fe Railroad & Heritage Museum.

GAINESVILLE (1901–1931)

By 1901, Gainesville, Texas, with a population of almost eight thousand, had become one of the state's major rail centers. A brick, Mission Revival–style building was constructed to house the Santa Fe depot, Harvey House

Santa Fe Station, Harvey House and Park in Gainesville, Texas. *Courtesy of Michael McMillan.*

Lunch Room and Newsstand. The architectural style is considered a "reinterpretation" of the Spanish Mission style of California. As was typical in these rural locations, there were living quarters upstairs for the Harvey House manager and Harvey Girls.

Gainesville was the last spot of civilization on a frequently traveled trail drive, making the town a wild, jumping-off point for cowboys herding cattle north into Indian Territory. These conditions brought a booming business for bars and prostitutes who usually lived (and worked) on the second floor of the saloon. This atmosphere is precisely what originally prompted Fred Harvey to establish his restaurants along the railroad. As passenger service developed on the Santa Fe, he realized there were no suitable arrangements for decent food for railroad travelers. Often, the local saloon served overpriced, barely edible beans and cornbread in surroundings particularly unsuitable for families and women traveling alone.

The Gainesville Harvey House gained a good reputation as a nice place to enjoy a delicious meal. Yet the lunchroom was not immune to the rough and rowdy ways of the time, and occasionally fights would erupt amid the linen and china. Unlike most Harvey House locations, Harvey Girls were not well received in this north Texas town primarily because of the stigma of living on the second floor of the depot. Women who worked in Gainesville as Harvey Girls were reluctant to discuss their experiences, which might explain why there is very little Gainesville Harvey Girl history. However, there is no question that this location delivered the expected Harvey standard of service, and Gainesville staff was held in high esteem.

Certainly manager P.J. Crozier was considered a well-respected Harvey employee as he was sent from Gainesville to open the restaurant in the new, fashionable El Ortiz Harvey Hotel in Lamy, New Mexico, fifteen miles southeast of the state capital, Santa Fe. Touring cars known as "Harveycars" provided transportation for train passengers from Lamy into Santa Fe because the Santa Fe Railroad did not lay tracks into the historic city. Some have speculated that local politics are to blame for this, while others believe the mountainous terrain was not suitable for building tracks to span the short distance from Lamy. However, there was a Harvey House in Santa Fe. In the mid-1920s, Fred Harvey's son Ford purchased the La Fonda hotel and transformed it into a Harvey showplace. The hotel, although no longer a Harvey establishment, remains a popular center of hospitality just off the Plaza in the center of Santa Fe.

The Fred Harvey company employed European chefs in most of its Harvey Houses, and this remote, often unrefined, location of Gainesville was no exception. Ernest Emil Schurig, who first worked at the Harvey House in Galveston, later became the chef in the Gainesville Lunch Room. The German-born chef brought his family to the United States, and he worked for Fred Harvey in several locations in Texas, Oklahoma and Colorado from 1911 until the 1940s.

Local water was considered unsuitable for making the famous Fred Harvey coffee, thus water had to be shipped from Fort Worth on the train. As with all Harvey Houses, meat was shipped direct from Kansas City, and fruit, poultry, eggs and milk were purchased locally when the food products met the Harvey standards.

Fundraising financed restoration of the depot where the Gainesville Harvey House was located, and the building is now home to the Santa Fe Depot Museum.

SOMERVILLE (1901–1940)

The Harvey House opened in Somerville, Texas, divisional headquarters of the Santa Fe Line, in 1901, the year Fred Harvey died. The building was a two-story, 260-foot-long galleried structure that contained a lunchroom, dining room, guest rooms and a newsstand. The Harvey House became the social center of the town and boosted the local economy. In 1913, the Somerville

Santa Fe Station, hotel and Harvey House in Somerville, Texas. *Courtesy of Michael McMillan.*

establishment was included in a special newspaper edition paying tribute to about twenty-five local businesses. The Harvey House was described as being among the popular and widely known eating houses in this part of the country. H.A. Rutter, manager at the time, had worked one year at the Hutchinson, Kansas Harvey House before relocating to Somerville.

The Harvey House was considered an ideal place for the accommodation of the traveling public and the officials of the Santa Fe railroad. The second floor had eight guest rooms and twenty-five rooms for Harvey and Santa Fe employees. The lunchroom seated twenty around a familiar Harvey House–style, horseshoe-shaped counter. The Somerville location was noted for a park containing trees and blooming flowers that was maintained by railroad worker John Schluens in his free time.

In February 1909, the *Somerville News Tribune* reported high expectations for a building boom "that is sure to follow the announcement by the Santa Fe of the erection of the new roundhouse." The roundhouse, an imposing building used for repairing train engines before the introduction of diesel fuel, also provided steam to heat the Harvey House, eliminating the need for individual coal stoves. During warm months, ceiling fans and open windows provided relief from the heat. A boiler outside near the back of the kitchen furnished hot water for the Harvey House.

Somerville was an exception to the Harvey procedure of providing printed menus from the Kansas City home office. One of the local staff was

Harvey Girls at the Harvey House lunch counter in Somerville, Texas. *Courtesy of ATSFry. com, R.L. Crump Library Collection, Copy and Reuse Restrictions Apply.*

responsible for hand printing and duplicating the menus, possibly because this was one of the smaller Harvey Houses in the system. The limited seating in the lunchroom and dining room proved to be inadequate when as many as seventy-five customers came ready to eat each time a train stopped.

The Harvey House in Somerville was, as in all rural locations, the best place to hold special events that included a meal. One event was described in the local newspaper as "a very enjoyable and pretty 7 o'clock, nine-course dinner." The menu included: "Tomato Bouillon en Tasse, Mixed Olives, Iced Cucumbers, Baked Filets of Red Fish Bordelaise, Potatoes Long Branch, Boiled Squab Chicken on Toast, French Peas, Special Baked Potatoes, Fruit Salad in Orange Baskets, Lemon Ice, Roquefort Cheese, Wafer Crackers and Black Coffee." The elaborate menu was most likely considered quite exotic in the small town of less than two thousand.

Special school functions, such as senior banquets, were usually held at the Somerville Harvey House. The local newspaper reported a banquet for the "home economic girls," which included the following menu: "Soup, Saltines, Tomato on Lettuce Leaf, Half of a Fried Chicken with Gravy, Olives, Buttered Rolls, Gherkins, New Potatoes, Vanilla Cream, Coffee, Iced

Tea, and Milk. At nine-thirty the girls and Miss Krenek departed from the Harvey House and went to the carnival to spend a few minutes."

Community business was often conducted at the Harvey House. In March 1935, the Boosters Club was organized there. About fifty people attended a meeting following a wholesome supper. The group was interested in promoting the building of State Highway 36 through Somerville.

In July 1929, "one of the largest social events ever given in Somerville was a going away picnic honoring Mrs. Ella White. Mrs. White has been manager of the Harvey House for the last ten years."

In every Harvey town, during the long, hectic hours of serving train passengers, there were bright spots. Perhaps a favorite railroad man would stop for a cup of delicious Fred Harvey coffee or someone more well known would occupy a stool at the lunch counter. Memorable Somerville Harvey Girl experiences include serving the Wayne King Orchestra in the mid-1920s on its way to perform in Houston.

Somerville Harvey Girls wore long black skirts and blouses covered with crisp white aprons with attached bibs. In the mid-1920s, a starched white collar and black bow tie were added to the uniform. Male managers and cashiers wore dark suits; female managers wore either black skirts and white blouses or white dresses. The kitchen staff wore white pants with jackets, the length of the jacket denoting difference in responsibilities.

Many Harvey employees were transferred to Somerville from Chicago or larger Harvey Houses in Kansas; however, with U.S. involvement in World War I, the establishment began hiring more locals. In addition to the Harvey Girl staff, a manager, two cashiers, a chef, a fry cook, a baker, a pastry cook, two dishwashers and a porter kept the Harvey House open twenty-four hours a day. Somerville residents employed at the restaurant included Adeline Balke, head waitress for twenty-two years, and Nello Strickland Sr., night cashier.

Leona Woods brought her extensive Harvey Girl experience to Somerville in 1935 following employment in Temple, Slaton, Brownwood and at the Grand Canyon. Leona recalled confusion in the dining room of the rural Texas towns when patrons first experienced small shallow finger bowls at each place setting. The bowls, filled with lemon water, were for diners to rinse their fingers between the multiple-course Harvey House dinners.

A thriving Harvey House was a benefit to the local economy in one sense. Although most meat was shipped in from Kansas City and dairy products came from the Harvey-owed dairy in Temple, fresh vegetables and eggs were purchased locally whenever possible. However, the cost of a meal at the

Harvey House was almost always less than in other local eateries, putting a strain on those businesses to keep customers coming in the door.

A remodel of the Somerville Harvey House was completed in 1925. The enlarged building was painted railroad-yellow with a red roof, white posts and banisters. Metal signs that extended from the building announced "Fred Harvey Lunch Room," and a brass gong imported from Hong Kong was brought outside and struck with a baseball attached to a stick to direct train passengers to their awaiting meals. The lunchroom now had two horseshoe-shaped counters that together seated up to forty people, as well as a dining room with eight large tables.

The closing of the Harvey House in 1940 was not a surprise to the staff or town residents. Personnel were notified in the early 1930s that the system was closing some of the restaurants and hotels due to the "effect of changing modes of travel." As steam was replaced with diesel, there was no longer a need for trains to stop every one hundred miles or so for coal. Dining cars were being added to the trains so passengers could eat while they traveled. Although the Harvey House enjoyed a robust business from Somerville locals, this was not enough to keep this location open.

After closing, the Somerville depot and Harvey House structure was remodeled into a one-story building that housed a freight and ticket office, yard offices, baggage room and express offices. The building was dismantled in 1943.

SILSBEE (1905–1923)

The depot was built in Silsbee, Texas, in 1902, approximately a year after the town became a stop on the Santa Fe Railroad. The Harvey House opened in 1905 with a full array of Harvey services: lunchroom, dining room, newsstand and hotel with a barbershop and poolroom in the basement. Unfortunately, the facility burned a year after opening. A new three-story, brick Harvey House with smaller eating facilities was completed in 1908 at a reported cost of $70,000. Fred Harvey continued to serve residents of Silsbee and train passengers in this building until 1923.

It was a tremendous task to furnish several million meals a year in Harvey Houses from Illinois to California and have one meal just as good as another, despite the diversity in climate and location. Put simply, whatever it took to ensure the freshest, highest quality food was done. When the menu said, "fresh orange juice," that is exactly what it meant. At the Harvey House,

Early photo of the train depot and Harvey House in Silsbee, Texas. *Courtesy of Ice House Museum, Silsbee, Texas.*

juice was squeezed after the customer ordered it. Storing it in the refrigerator for use later was not allowed. Prompted by concern over the exposure of milk stored in open containers to bacteria, Harvey dairies were among the first in the country to use sealed milk bottles.

Following are annual food quantities for existing Harvey Houses put forth in a 1907 company report: 300,000 pounds of butter; 500,000 pounds of ham; 100,000 pounds of bacon; 150,000 pounds of lard; 300,000 pounds of coffee; 1,000,000 pounds of sugar; 800,000 pounds of potatoes; and 6,480,000 eggs. As a frame of reference, at this time, only nine of the sixteen Harvey restaurants were operating in Texas.

About ten years after the Silsbee Harvey House opened, Della Husband moved there from Lee's Mill, a small community in Newton County, the easternmost county of Texas. While performing her duties as a Harvey Girl, she met and married E.E. Dunbar, a brakeman for the Gulf, Colorado and Santa Fe Railroad. Della's brother Hugh P. Husband worked for Fred Harvey as a bookkeeper.

In the early 1920s, Robert Otis Thomas, who began as a cashier at the Harvey House in Silsbee, transferred to the Somerville, Texas establishment and later became manager of the Harvey House in Galveston (1929–36). Thomas, in a conversation relayed by Galveston Harvey Girl Madge Saenz, explained how the Harvey system maintained consistent food quality in Harvey Houses. All operations were controlled in the main office in Kansas City, Missouri, from personnel policies to food service. All managers were

Left: Madge Saenz, former Galveston Harvey Girl, was honored in 1990 when a historical marker was installed at the Harvey House site in Silsbee, Texas. *Courtesy of Raymond Saenz.*

Below: Harvey Girls in the Lunch Room in Silsbee, Texas. *Courtesy of Northern Arizona University, Cline Library, Fred Harvey Collection.*

trained in Kansas City, and in the early days of the system, most potential Harvey Girls went there for personal interviews. Manuals containing recipes with detailed instructions for food preparation, including the garnish for special dishes, were issued to each Harvey House. After the death of Fred Harvey, Harvey House managers were considered his living extension. Continuing the Harvey tradition of courtesy and service, while train passengers were dining the Harvey manager would circulate through the room announcing, "Passengers have plenty of time. Ample notice will be given before departure of the train."

A letter written by former Silsbee Harvey Girl Nellie Darrow to *Santa Fe Magazine* tells us a great deal about the working environment that was common in Fred Harvey establishments. Nellie wrote, in part, "I am in the service of Fred Harvey as a waitress, having first been employed at Silsbee, Tex. While there I was treated as well as any young woman could wish to be treated and I found among the railroad boys many true, stanch friends, whose good wishes I hope always to retain." Further relating her story, Darrow states that while working at her last location on the Harvey system in Temple, Texas, she became very ill. "What did the dear little cashier at the Harvey House do but start a subscription to send me to a resort for treatment, and in one day she had secured enough to allow me to remain at the resort for twenty-five days and to take twenty-one baths." After expressing her sincere appreciation to fellow employees who so kindly provided for her during this time of need, Nellie concluded, "I have been offered a position elsewhere but I surely would feel lost in any place but a Harvey House."

AMARILLO (1910–1940)

Realizing the need to extend railroad service farther north, the Santa Fe considered several routes through the Texas Panhandle, most passing south of Amarillo. However, the company decided it would not be wise to "leave out a live town like Amarillo if we can conveniently take it in." Quickly, the town grew into one of the world's busiest cattle-shipping points, and in ten years, the population had grown from 482 to almost 2,000.

In 1910, a large brick, Mission Revival–style Santa Fe passenger station and Harvey House were built, similar in style to the Gainesville, Texas site. The Fred Harvey company brought a lunchroom, dining room and newsstand to Amarillo, along with a legion of smiling Harvey Girls.

Santa Fe Railroad Station and Harvey House in Amarillo, Texas. *Courtesy of Amarillo Public Library.*

Gleaming coffee urns, desserts displayed under glass domes and fresh fruit greeted diners in the Amarillo, Texas Harvey House Lunch Room. *Courtesy of Special Collections/University of Arizona Library/Fred Harvey: Traveling the Rails in Grand Style collection.*

According to an interview printed in a Santa Fe employee newsletter in 1952, the excitement of the trains arriving and departing at the Amarillo Santa Fe Depot stirred Harvey Girl Opal Sells's imagination. The depot filled with train passengers several times a day, and she imagined the many places these travelers would visit. For now, though, the challenge in front of her was learning the "Harvey Girl" way. The Harvey House manager, Mr. Lindsey, had been very kind; however, he made it clear that there were good reasons for the rules a Harvey Girl was required to follow. Some of the rules were not much different from what Momma had expected of Opal at home: Be courteous and respectful. Only speak when spoken to. However, remembering exactly how to place the knife and fork or on which side to serve the food to a customer wasn't as easy to remember. Fred Harvey's name was etched in the handle of the silverware and was a constant reminder of her employer's expectations.

This newest Harvey Girl in Amarillo had grown up on a farm not far outside of town, and even in that rural setting, Opal had been expected to maintain a "proper" appearance. The Harvey rules that didn't allow makeup, required her to keep her hair neat and to always wear clean, crisply ironed dresses just came naturally. That's what Opal had always done. However, the table setting in the farm kitchen that Opal and her mother shared was very simple compared to the Harvey House dining room, and their meals were certainly not as elaborate. Opal had never eaten—much less served—a five-course meal before.

The youngest of seven children, Opal had stayed home to care for her invalid mother. After her mother's death, the family was certain that Opal, now in her mid-twenties, had missed her opportunity to find a husband. A charitable uncle paid her tuition to a business college, where she received secretarial training. However, it didn't take Opal long to realize that a career as a stenographer was not for her.

An acquaintance suggested that Opal apply to work at the Harvey House. This possibility appealed to her sense of propriety, and she knew that if she worked hard, she would have the opportunity to move to other Harvey Houses down the Santa Fe line. "So I went in to see a manager at the Harvey House in Amarillo. He said to me, 'You're the first girl who has walked in here today who wasn't chewing gum. You look like our type.' He hired me that day, and I began work the next morning. I was real nervous."

Even though Opal longed for the adventure of traveling west as a Harvey Girl, there were exciting experiences in Amarillo. She served businessmen from Chicago and moneyed couples headed to the hot springs at the

Montezuma Hotel, a Fred Harvey establishment in Las Vegas, New Mexico. She saw Will Rogers, famous cowboy humorist, in Amarillo, where he would draw a crowd downtown with rope tricks and storytelling. "He was a frequent passenger on the Santa Fe in the 1920s. When he came into the Harvey House, everybody knew what he wanted to eat and he was served what he wanted, even at dinner time." (Normally, diners had to choose from two or three entrees offered on the menu.).Three years later, Opal Sells was leaving the familiar surroundings of the Texas Panhandle to work at the Bisonte, a Harvey hotel in Hutchinson, Kansas. From there, she was sent to the Union Terminal in Cleveland, Ohio, where she worked in the posh Fred Harvey restaurant called the English Oak Room. In 1933, Opal worked as a Harvey Girl in the tearoom located in the Straus Building at the Chicago World's Fair.

Years later, Opal settled in Albuquerque, New Mexico, and worked at the Alvarado Hotel there, ending her career with Fred Harvey as cashier in the Alvarado Coffee Shop. During a career with the Fred Harvey company that spanned forty-five years, Opal worked in ten different Harvey establishments. While at the Alvarado, she married John S. Hill, who had been employed by the Santa Fe Railroad for the same number of years as Opal had been employed by Fred Harvey.

Desree Arrowood also began her career at the Amarillo Harvey House and took advantage of the opportunity to travel. Remembering her Harvey Girl days, Desree wrote, "In 1929 I hired out at the Amarillo, Texas Harvey House and was transferred to Waynoka, Oklahoma in 1930." Next Desree went to Emporia, Kansas, for a short time and then to Dodge City, Kansas. She was then "lucky enough to be chosen to go to Newton, Kansas when the new house opened there." Desree shared the feeling most other young women had about working as a Harvey Girl. "It was very exciting. Times were hard and I felt I was very lucky in more than one way. We had a nice place to live, a good house mother and good managers." Desree left her Harvey House employ when she married in 1933. The newlyweds traveled by train to honeymoon at the Chicago World's Fair.

The strict Harvey Girl rules stayed with the women throughout their lives. "To this day, I can't stand to see a knife blade pointing outward," said Vernon Downes, who was quoted in a mid-1980s *Los Angeles Times* article. Downes worked at the Amarillo Harvey House with Opal Sells. "It's a very tiny thing, a small thing, but when they throw the silver down in front of you, I just can't stand that. A lot of things I notice now, even in a real nice place—like where the glass of water goes, the bread and butter dish, the silver. They just

The Santa Fe Orchestra was composed of railroad and Harvey House employees in Amarillo, Texas, circa 1930. *Courtesy of Gray's Studio, Amarillo, Texas.*

put them any place. They don't know where they go. Old as I am, and it's been many years, I still remember." Vernon Downes felt that being a Harvey Girl was "a lot like going away to school." She described living in nicely furnished rooms over the station, much like a dorm, two girls in each room. But most schoolgirls didn't have daily inspections as the Harvey Girls did. "We actually stood inspection before going on the floor," Downes recalled. "Our shoes must be shined, not too much makeup, uniform must be neat and clean. They didn't stand for any foolishness."

Harvey and Santa Fe employees left their imprint in rural Texas communities in a variety of ways. For example, train conductors for the Santa Fe changed forever the way "Amarillo" was pronounced. Early-day pronunciation was loyal to the Spanish: Ah-mah-REE-yoh, meaning "yellow." However as conductors passed through passenger cars, the town's name became: Am-ah-RILL-ow. Actually, the name of this Santa Fe town proved to be a challenge in other ways. The original sign on the first depot misspelled this Texas Panhandle stop, displaying in bold letters: Amarilla.

C.W. Weber, who began his tenure as manager in 1928, found time to organize an orchestra of Amarillo Harvey and Santa Fe employees. This intimate group of thirty musicians most certainly provided an opportunity for employees to relax and to interact with the community. The symphony performed public concerts on the eleventh floor of the Santa Fe Building. The stage curtain was decorated with the Santa Fe logo, and a felt banner displayed the name: Santa Fe Orchestra.

When there weren't enough employees and railroaders to make up a performing orchestra, Weber recruited musicians from the community. Irving Tolzien, who owned Tolzien's Music Store, played for both the Santa Fe Orchestra and the Amarillo Symphony, which was founded in 1924. Willard Smith also performed with Weber's orchestra. Smith certainly brought experience to the group—he performed with John Philip Sousa's band during World War I. It appears that the constant movement of Harvey employees between locations might have proved to be a challenge to the orchestra conductor. A list of musicians accompanying an orchestra photograph in September 1932 differs quite a bit from a list of May 1932 musicians.

E.L. Lindsey was manager of the Amarillo Harvey House in 1925, and Afton Lindsey took over the position in 1927. In 1936, C.M. Gunther, with twenty-five years' experience, came to Amarillo from Syracuse, Kansas, to succeed C.V. McDaniels as manager of the Harvey House. McDaniels was moved to the Harvey House in Bakersfield, California. Soon after his arrival in Amarillo, Gunther was interviewed for the local newspaper and stated these were "the food faults that the average person objects to with the most gusto: over-seasoned food, dishes that are under seasoned, hot food and cold dishes served lukewarm." Mr. Gunther was described as having "made his living by pleasing the public. His experience has taught him what it likes and what it dislikes the most." Gunther believed that "as a general rule people are not hard to please—if they get what they pay for. If they don't—well!" In Mr. Gunther's opinion, most men liked apple pie for dessert, while women preferred some type of light frozen dessert. He said, "Courtesy is the cheapest thing in the restaurant business and it means the most."

In the interview, Mr. Gunther also provided insight into the travelers of the time: "The casual traveler has a constant fear of getting left. He presents an amusing sight as he crams and bolts his food in his effort to get back on the train. On the other hand, the experienced traveler sitting at his side will serenely munch his food, stroll leisurely to his train and sit down by his fast-eating friend who is now sighing with relief because he made the train."

The Amarillo Harvey House and Santa Fe Depot building was privately owned for years and is well preserved. Much of the interior of the depot remains the same as when the Harvey House was operating, including a separate "colored" waiting room adjacent to the main depot waiting room.

The large stained-glass windows still in place in the dining room area are particularly reminiscent of the Harvey heydays.

An original telegraph receiver has been preserved. This was a key piece of equipment in all Harvey House operations. Conductors would take food orders from passengers on the train and telegraph the information to the depot. When passengers were seated in the Harvey House, their steaming hot meals, made to order, were placed before them.

The Amarillo depot and Harvey House building was purchased by the City of Amarillo in 2013. The city council stated, "It is important to protect the historic structure that could figure into downtown redevelopment."

CANADIAN (1910–1939)

The Canadian Harvey House was a red brick, two-story building with a tiled roof connected to the passenger depot by a covered walkway. Built in the Prairie style, the attractive building, eighty feet long and twenty-four feet wide, had strong horizontal lines emphasized with crisp white trim and many windows to allow for ample light and cross-ventilation. A full basement contained a boiler room and storage room where dry and canned foods were kept. In addition to the eating areas, the ground floor had a large kitchen with two large walk-in refrigerators and a pantry as well as stoves, ovens, grills, a steamer and a broiler. All bread, pastries, cookies, cakes and pies were made in the bakery. Double swinging doors led to the lunchroom and dining room. The cost to build the structure in 1910 was $30,000.

Even this remote, north Texas location enforced Fred Harvey's "coat rule," requiring male Harvey House patrons to wear a coat if they were eating in the dining room. The requirement was challenged in 1921 by the Corporate Commission of the State of Oklahoma. The commission claimed it showed discrimination among patrons; however, the appellate court ordered this decision overturned, and the coat rule stood. Most Harvey House managers had a few dark coats in various sizes set aside to accommodate a gentleman diner who arrived coatless. A man having to wear a coat while eating a meal, even in warm weather, must have seemed silly to some in remote rural towns, and enforcing the coat rule was surely a challenge when cowboys showed up carrying guns.

Canadian Harvey Girls who worked in the lunchroom wore black blouses and white skirts with a pinafore-style front and double straps in

Santa Fe Station and Harvey House in Canadian, Texas. The building of similar architecture on the left of the image is the Santa Fe Reading Room. *Courtesy of Michael McMillan.*

back, white starched collar and cuffs and a black, loose bow tie. Those serving in the dining room wore white blouses and skirts with a black tie. Soiled uniforms, along with used linen tablecloths and napkins from the restaurant, were shipped in large canvas baskets by train to Topeka, Kansas, where they were laundered and returned the next day. Those large baskets served another, very different purpose when hunters from the Midwest and East came to Canadian to hunt prairie chicken and quail. A busboy remembered helping clean "as much as two hundred pounds of prairie chicken" that were then packed in ice in the laundry baskets and shipped home on the train with the hunters.

Harvey Girls weren't the only Harvey employees with a strict dress code. Warren Harrington was a busboy at the Canadian Harvey House between 1929 and 1932 during summer vacations and after school. He remembered wearing white or black trousers, a white shirt, a white jacket and a black bow tie. At this time, before roads were paved, all of the county's wheat and livestock were shipped out from the depot. Harrington recalled two to four meal trains stopping each day. "I was responsible for spotting the trains and alerting the chef and the [Harvey] girls. I'd stand out on the platform where I could see up the tracks about four miles. With the first glimpse of the train, I would run back and report to the chef and then I would grab this big brass gong and whack the daylights out of it with a wood stick with a ball on the end of it." In the following twenty to thirty minutes, the cooks and Harvey Girls served about eighty passengers before the train continued on its way.

The busboy's verbal warning to the Harvey House staff allowed them to make final preparations for the passengers. The manager would have already been alerted by telegraph as to the number of guests to expect and their food choices.

Warren's siblings also worked many years for Fred Harvey. Both of his brothers were chefs and worked in many different Harvey House locations, including the Grand Canyon hotels. Two of his sisters were Harvey Girls. During his employment in Canadian, Warren also had the responsibility of serving the "colored" porters and conductors in an alcove that was just for them. Warren said, "They weren't allowed in the Lunch Room in those days."

Maxine Cockrell, who lived with her parents and fourteen siblings on a ranch south of Canadian, used a connection with a family friend to get a job at the Harvey House in 1935 when she was sixteen years old. Only the manager and the cook were allowed to be married, and Harvey Girls were not supposed to date, but that was one Harvey rule meant to be broken. Maxine enjoyed her responsibilities and found the work exciting. Before long, local cowboy Harold Wilson was courting the pretty brunette. They married in 1937 and decided to go to California, selling Harold's horse for traveling money. Once they learned Maxine was going to have a baby, they came back home so their child would be born a native Texan. Many years later, their grown son remarked, "I am forever grateful to them for it."

Elizabeth Hazelwood was a first-generation American when she was brought by her parents to Oklahoma in a covered wagon in 1899. She was two years old, and her father, a Russian immigrant, had come with his family from South Dakota to try farming farther south. He heard many promising things about Texas and moved to a farm outside Canadian. Farming in Texas was not as advertised, and soon the children, four girls and one boy, moved into town to find work. Elizabeth married at age eighteen and had two children before she was widowed ten years later. She was supporting her family as a café waitress in Canadian when she heard there was a better job at the Harvey House.

At the Canadian Harvey House, few women were sent from other locations to work, and more local women were hired, many of them married. Single women were required to live in the Harvey House dormitory-style living quarters; however, married women were allowed to maintain their own homes.

Harvey Girl Maxine Cockrell and local cowboy Harold F. Wilson in Canadian, Texas. The couple married and moved to California, but they returned to Texas so their first child would be born in their native state. *Courtesy of Spec Wilson.*

For a widow with small children, working as a Harvey Girl offered security and the support of an extended family. Elizabeth's daughter remembers her visits to the Harvey House every day after school when she and her brother waited for their mother to leave work. The proximity of the Harvey House to the railroad tracks and the busy rush when a train arrived was exciting to the children but caused their mother to worry for their safety.

Una Gertrude Atchison Matthews worked at the Canadian Harvey House in 1925. After her mother died, Una's father left her with her grandmother and came to Texas looking for work. In 1923, he took a job with the Santa Fe bridge gang in Canadian and, after meeting a woman he wanted to marry, sent for his family to join him in Canadian. "There were a lot of ranches here," Una remembered, "and a lot of cowboys. I was eighteen when my father's job in Canadian ended and my family decided to move on, but I wanted to stay. I had met a cowboy at the skating rink that winter, so after graduation I got a job at the Harvey House and worked all summer there. In the fall I got married, but I went on working just the same." Una and her husband, Bill, lived in a house in town, and Una walked to work until December when, without a car, the weather made this difficult. "I was working the night shift and Bill finally said, 'Quit!' and I did."

Alma Vera Allen Smith grew up in Canadian, graduated from high school in 1934 and soon after took a job as a Harvey Girl at the Canadian Harvey House. In a letter to the author, Alma wrote, "We had our stations to take care of—which included eight customers. Our side work was to see that the set ups were in order and everything neat and clean. This was during the

Dust Bowl days and it was real hard to keep the counters clean. We had to know all of the prices on the menu, which changed daily." Alma had good memories of her Harvey Girl days, saying, "It was a fun place to work and even with the hard work I enjoyed every minute of it." She worked three trains a day and lived at the Harvey House. "I roomed with the Head Waitress. My salary was one dollar a day and, of course, the tips I made were real good." Alma's years at the Harvey House were during the Depression, but with free room and board, "we really had a good living. The Harvey Girls lived on the first floor and the boys lived on the second floor. We had maid service and our uniforms were laundered for us. If we wanted to go anywhere in the evening we had to have a pass signed by the manager and had to be in by 10:00." Harvey employees enjoyed holiday parties that were well supervised. "We had a real good manager and his wife, Mr. & Mrs. Bobo." Mr. Bobo must have approved of Alma as well. He offered her a job as head waitress in the Needles, Arizona Harvey House. "I didn't take it and I have always wondered if I would have liked it. But time marches on!" Alma considered the Canadian Harvey House an exciting place to work. "The uniforms were real cute. We wore the black blouse during the week and a white one on Sunday with real cute button-on skirts. Our uniforms had to be spotless, and we had to wear hair nets at all times."

As efficient as Harvey operations were, things were hectic when a trainload of hungry passengers was expected. Alma wrote: "The first day I worked someone left a bucket of syrup sitting on the floor and the lid was not on very good. In my rush, I didn't see it and knocked the bucket over. I had an awful mess to clean up and after that I was more careful and watched where I was walking." Marshall Steele, a Harvey House baker, was transferred to Canadian from Newton, Kansas. Alma said, "We met, soon fell in love and got married." Apparently the Harvey rule to not date—much less marry—a fellow Harvey employee was no longer enforced. Alma and Marshall decided to leave their Harvey House jobs and move to Oklahoma because they wanted a place of their own.

George Hill was a night shift cook at the Canadian Harvey House in the early 1930s. These work hours put him on the job at the time the 3:28 a.m. passenger train stopped with a load of supplies. Very few items were bought locally. Dairy products came from Newton, Kansas, as did all poultry. Meat came from several sources, always in boxes packed with ice and rock salt. George also received the fresh laundry, some from Albuquerque and other times from Newton. Hill worked at the Waynoka, Oklahoma Harvey House before coming to Canadian. He failed his first test to become a cook because the wiener he fried cracked

Above: Hand-tinted postcard of the Harvey House Lunch Room in Canadian, Texas. *Courtesy of Michael McMillan.*

Left: Harvey Girl Maxine Cockrell, age seventeen, in Canadian, Texas. *Courtesy of Spec Wilson.*

open; later, he learned to successfully cook wieners in olive oil. George is credited with adding a thin slice of orange as garnish for ham and egg orders in the Harvey House. He also perfected a pancake mix he called "Quickie-Mix" that was eventually packaged for all Harvey Houses to use.

The head baker at the Canadian Harvey restaurant was from Germany and known only as Frank. His workday began at 4:00 a.m., and he was responsible for all the bread, rolls, cakes, donuts and pies. Certainly, Frank's freshly baked bread made the box lunches a favorite. For fifty cents, you would get two sandwiches—roast beef, ham or cheese—a slice of cake or piece of pie, a dill pickle and either an apple, orange or banana. The box lunches were especially popular with the Santa Fe employees leaving on a "run." Often when the train stopped in Canadian, there would be a prison car at the end, and the Harvey House provided a box lunch for each guard and prisoner, along with five gallons of coffee. This rail car came out of Chicago and was rumored to be picking up prisoners for Alcatraz. Harvey employees remembered that it was usually full.

In 1956, the Canadian Harvey House was sold and torn down for salvage. Doyle Wilson, a Canadian carpenter, bought the structure from the Santa Fe Railway Company for $2,000. The carpenter was given eighteen months to tear down and salvage approximately 200,000 bricks, plus lumber and other building materials. Prior to Wilson's acquisition, the building had remained vacant and unused since the Harvey House closed on June 15, 1939.

SWEETWATER (1911–1933)

The Harvey House that opened in Sweetwater, Texas, in 1911 was very different in structure and location from other Texas Harvey Houses. The Santa Fe was the last of four railroads to reach Nolan County, beginning operation through Sweetwater on December 27, 1910. Until 1918, the town name was spelled "Sweet Water" after nearby Sweet Water Creek. The Harvey building in town was constructed of wood painted dark green, trimmed in white with a red ceramic roof and was smaller than most of Fred Harvey's restaurants. However, there was space for a Harvey Newsstand with the latest newspapers and magazines for sale. A lumberman who obtained some of the lumber when the building was demolished used it in several houses he built in Sweetwater and remembered that the wood was first class, "not having a knot hole in the whole lot."

Harvey House Lunch Room and Newsstand in Sweetwater, Texas. *Courtesy of Michael McMillan.*

Adjacent to the restaurant was a two-story building that provided living quarters for employees of the Harvey House. Male employees lived upstairs and the Harvey Girls downstairs. The complex also included a three-story building where railroad workers could spend the night.

The Harvey House complex was north of Sweetwater, outside of the town on the main railroad track, and the Santa Fe Depot, designed by Kansas City architect Louis Curtiss, was near the center of town. Trains would back up in front of the Harvey House on a spur line, let passengers get off and then the train would continue backing into the depot to pick up freight and other passengers. Then, moving forward now, the train would return to the Harvey House, pick up the passengers, who had, by that time, finished their meals, and continue on its way.

Ruth Norville Newton worked at the Sweetwater Harvey House for a short time and remembers the long walks when she and other Harvey Girls went into town to shop. She said, "Nobody could afford a car in those days on the salaries we made." Ruth had just graduated from high school when she was hired to work in the restaurant. As she recalled, "Mr. Robert O. Thomas was manager while I was there. He was nice, and this was a good place for my first job. We lived in nice quarters." Ruth remembered watching the people get off the train and come into the lunchroom. "I wondered about their destination; many looked well off." As a young girl, she thought it would be wonderful to travel like the passengers she served. Later in life, she wrote in a letter, "Now I have been half way around

the world! Not in my wildest dreams did I ever think I would be able to travel like that when I was working as a Harvey Girl." Ruth also worked in the Harvey House in the Houston Union Station. "I transferred to Houston so I could work while I was attending Business College. It was there that I met and married a railroad official. We traveled a great deal before his death in 1969. I never remarried as I had such a happy life I was afraid it would be pushing my luck to have more than one good husband in a life time [*sic*]."

Just like in Harvey House communities everywhere, the citizens of Sweetwater enjoyed eating at the local Harvey restaurant. Margaret Hill remembered that when she was a child, her father, Mose Newman, would take her to the Harvey House for breakfast every Sunday morning. She was quite impressed by the food, her surroundings and the Harvey Girl uniforms, including "the big white bows in their hair."

Top: Harvey Girl Ethel Reeves Tate, circa 1925 in Sweetwater, Texas. *Courtesy of Slaton Railroad Heritage Association.*

Left: Joe W. Tate, Harvey House kitchen staff, Slaton, Texas, circa 1919. *Courtesy of Slaton Railroad Heritage Association.*

Ethel Reeves came to Sweetwater in the mid-1920s to work as a Harvey Girl after seeing an ad in the Somerville Post Office. According to her daughter Jolene Fondy, one day while her mother was working in the lunchroom, a railroad man, Joe Tate, came in. "My mother said, 'That's the best looking man I've ever seen, and I'm going to marry him.'" Ethel's proclamation came true when the couple married in Slaton, Texas, a year or so later, and her Harvey Girl career ended. Tate began working at age sixteen as a busboy in the Slaton Harvey House, and once he turned twenty-one, he was hired by the Santa Fe Railroad. "My daddy continued to work for the Santa Fe and was sent to California," Jolene explained. "I can remember riding the train back home and eating at Harvey Houses along the way—Needles and Barstow, California, and Winslow, Arizona. They were so nice, and the food was always good."

Fred Harvey's business acumen is intricately woven through our country's history, and many families have fond Harvey House memories. The following story accompanied an article about Harvey Houses published in a travel magazine in the early 1990s. During the Depression, a mother was driving with her son and daughter to meet her husband, who had gone ahead to find work. About halfway to their destination, it became obvious there was not enough money for gas and food. The mother stopped at a Harvey House and explained her situation to the Harvey Girl, who summoned the manager. The writer of this story was the young boy, and many years later, he remembered that, although his mother asked only for a sandwich for the children and a cup of coffee for herself, the manager suggested that she allow him to order food for the family. After asking the Harvey Girl to bring the family hot soup, beef stew, milk, hot chocolate and cobbler "all around," he added, "and these people are the guests of Mr. Fred Harvey."

"The taste of the rich brown stew is still with me. And thinking about it still brings up the picture of that immense restaurant, so clean it looked as if it had been polished, and the waitresses, the Harvey Girls, with their bright smiles, puffed sleeves and starched aprons," the man remembered. As the family left, the Harvey Girl handed two bags to the mother, saying, "The manager said I was to wrap up what you didn't eat so you could take it along." The boy protested, explaining that they had "cleaned their plates," but his mother gratefully picked up the sacks. "In the car, my mother and sister looked in the bags, which clearly contained more food than we'd had for dinner." The boy asked, "What's in them?" His mother said, "Loaves and fishes."

The Harvey way of doing business continued as the company expanded in Texas. Whenever possible, food was bought locally, which provided the freshest ingredients for the delicious meals and also contributed to the local economy. Luther Pence remembered when he was a boy walking across the bridge at Kildugan Creek near Sweetwater to sell a bucket of eggs and several pounds of freshly churned butter to the Harvey House. During the Depression years, helping supply food for the local Harvey House was surely beneficial to the local farmers.

Passenger service to Sweetwater was discontinued in the early 1960s, and the Fred Harvey buildings north of the town were torn down in the early 1970s.

SLATON (1912–1942)

There's no question that Slaton, Texas, was, from its very beginning, a railroad town. In the early 1900s, passenger service on the Santa Fe Railroad was booming, and the company needed a division point to service trains traveling through northwest Texas. There was no town at the point along the tracks to meet this need. In 1911, the Santa Fe Railway purchased the land on which the town of Slaton was built. The first residents lived in tents while carpenters were building small frame buildings. The Slaton Santa Fe complex developed into the center of the largest division in the Santa Fe system.

The streets of Slaton were designed in the shape of a wagon wheel with the city hall in the hub. One of the "spokes" was named Railroad Avenue, and it pointed straight from the center of town to the new Harvey House and Santa Fe Depot. In a design often used by the Santa Fe during this time, the Mission Revival–style Harvey House opened in Slaton in 1912 at a cost of $75,000. The restaurant seated forty-two people around a large oval counter with a rose-colored marble top. The newsstand and gift shop opened into the eating area, and the kitchen and bakery were tucked behind wooden swinging doors.

The Fred Harvey company hired educated women of good character, and when these employees moved into the small towns in Texas, their positive influence had a long-term impact on the communities. As the town of Slaton developed, Harvey Girls helped organize quilting bees, taught Sunday school and helped develop an appreciation for art and music in the small town.

Fannie Belle Green came to Slaton with the railroad. She had been a Harvey Girl at the Vaughn, New Mexico Harvey House before transferring to Slaton in 1912 to help establish the new location. Living in the dormitory-style residence of Harvey Houses must have seemed particularly luxurious to Fannie. Born in Bowie County, Texas, her family moved to Indian Territory in

Hand-tinted postcard of the Harvey House in Slaton, Texas. *Courtesy of Michael McMillan.*

Harvey Girls (from left) Bertha Garragus, Patsy Hoffman, Grace Squires, Cleo Wolf and Alma Russell in Slaton, Texas. *Courtesy of Slaton Railroad Heritage Association.*

1899, where home was a half-dugout on the flat prairie. By the early 1900s, her father relocated his extended family to remote Encino, New Mexico, where he worked as a carpenter. A female railroad agent at Vaughn, fifteen miles away, persuaded Fannie, her sister and a cousin to become Harvey Girls.

Grace Squires (in cart) with unidentified Harvey Girls in Slaton, Texas. *Courtesy of Slaton Railroad Heritage Association.*

Although a remote railroad location, Vaughn had its share of excitement, including a visit by Charles Lindbergh, who made an emergency landing in the desolate New Mexico desert and spent time at the Harvey House. However, Fannie was pleased with her transfer to the new Slaton Harvey House, where she found it more exciting with more railroaders and fewer rowdy cowboys.

Serving customers in a Harvey House was a natural fit for Fannie. At age seven, when her mother became ill, Fannie cooked and served her first meal to men who were helping with the harvest. Although a chef and kitchen staff handled food preparation in the Harvey House, in Slaton, Fannie and the other four waitresses on the day shift were responsible for keeping Harvey coffee freshly made. The Harvey Girls had to memorize orders and pass them on to the cooks, who committed them to memory and rang a bell when the food was ready. A notepad kept in an apron pocket was used only to total the cost of each meal for the cashier.

The day shift began at 7:00 every morning and, after serving passengers from three trains plus railroad employees and local diners, ended at 6:00 p.m. A normal workday allowed for a two-hour break in the afternoon, and unless there was a shortage of Harvey Girls, everyone was allowed one day off each week.

Left: Former Harvey Girl Rose Hielers Farschon, age eighty-eight, re-created her Harvey uniform for a special celebration at the Slaton, Texas Harvey House in 2005. *Courtesy of Slaton Railroad Heritage Association.*

Below: Group photo of Fred Harvey company employees at the Harvey House in Slaton, Texas. Harvey Girl Cleo Wolf is the fifth person from the left, back row. *Courtesy of Slaton Railroad Heritage Association.*

Fannie's social life might have been tame by some Harvey Girl standards. She usually went to the Santa Fe Reading Room next door to the Harvey House where an assortment of reading material was provided for train passengers and railroad employees. As Fannie strolled across the brick promenade to the Reading Room, she began to take notice of Joe Teague Jr., the night ticket agent, as he walked to work each evening. Soon Joe began to come to work early so there was some time to talk to Fannie, and their time off from work was coordinated as often as possible. Fannie's Harvey Girl career ended in 1915 when she and Joe married. The couple continued to live in Slaton, and the Teague family established the Teague Confectionary. The business, later named Teague Drug, remained a center of commerce and community socialization on the downtown square in Slaton until 1987.

While spending the summer of 1936 in Slaton with her aunt, twenty-one-year-old Mary Rosina "Rose" Hielers heard there was an opening for a waitress at the Harvey House. Her Aunt Mattie recommended Rose for the job, and she was hired. Rose left her home and most of her family in Stratton, Nebraska, to become a Harvey Girl.

As with most Harvey Girls, Rose discovered working for Fred Harvey was a pleasant experience and was much more rewarding than her job as a sales clerk in the general merchandise store in Nebraska. Her hours there had been long, and the pay was meager. At the Harvey House, all of the employees were congenial, and the family atmosphere made being so far from home much easier. There were about twenty employees at this restaurant and newsstand, including the manager and his wife. The Harvey Girls lived on the second floor, and the manager's wife acted as their house mother. Male employees lived in a separate building.

A job at the Harvey House was a special blessing, as jobs of any kind for women were hard to find in the mid-1930s. The young women were paid one dollar a day plus tips and received free room and board. They also enjoyed laundry service and received a pass to ride the Santa Fe anywhere in the United States. All of these benefits plus her salary were equal to twice as much as Rose's previous income. "To be a Harvey Girl, you had to have good morals and be reasonably attractive," Rose said. "You had to be modest and well mannered." She also explained that a little bit of lip color was the only makeup allowed, and jewelry was not allowed. Rose met Bill Farschon, a train dispatcher, on a blind date. They were married over sixty years before Bill passed away in 2001.

Other Slaton Harvey girls included: Cleo Wolf, 1924–32; Irene Wolf, 1920–22; Hermein Kroll, 1939; Isabell Hill, 1936–38; and Zula Mae

Bownds, whose employment dates are not recorded. Hill remembers that waitresses were like sisters to one another, and most of the employees felt that they had a family with the Fred Harvey operation. Sharing living quarters on the second floor of the Harvey House certainly added to the family atmosphere. Cleo Wolf explained the Harvey procedure for hiring Harvey Girls. "They didn't go out and hire someone off the street. You were screened very carefully as to character and reputation."

Cleo also recalled filling any free time by polishing the huge silver urns and silverware: "They had to be polished to perfection. The linen napkins had to be folded 'just so' and ready to use." Wolf remembered when a group from a foreign country visited the Slaton Harvey House, and she had trouble understanding their orders: "A man asked for a bottle of milk and I thought he said buttermilk. It took the manager to get things straightened out." When a trainload of passengers swooped into the Harvey House, things were hectic. Wolf related the story of rushing into one of the large swinging doors between the dining room and kitchen carrying a tray of food. The manager was stooped over looking into the linen cabinet, and "of course, I knocked him over, but I didn't drop the tray! I was a farm girl from a quiet town, and the buzzing activity of the Harvey House seemed exciting to me. I met many people from every walk of life as that was the most popular mode of travel at that time."

The uniforms of the Harvey Girls have been romanticized, everyone in black blouses and skirts with white, starched aprons. The reality, as Wolf remembered, was how very stiff and hot the uniforms were. "And without air conditioning, it was very uncomfortable during warm weather."

Bert Polk was a cook at the Slaton Harvey House from 1933 to 1940. His duties ranged from stocking supplies and clearing tables to assisting with the cooking and baking. Polk was also responsible for ringing a bell in front of the restaurant to attract train passengers disembarking at the depot, several railcars away. He remembered, "We had good cooks all of the time. There were maybe eighteen to twenty employees, and I was the first one to work nights."

Calvin Lamb was hired in 1941 as a busboy at the Slaton Harvey House. He was in high school and worked during the summer, on weekends and occasionally at night. Busboy responsibilities were varied, depending on the time of day. "I washed dishes, cleaned the floor and did whatever they asked me to do," Lamb said in a recent telephone conversation. "The restaurant was open twenty-four hours a day. I remember one time when the night cook wanted to go on vacation, and they had me fill in. I mostly fed the train crews, and they weren't very particular. That was probably a good thing." Lamb explained that a truck from the nearby round house (Santa Fe facility where train

Slaton, Texas Harvey House staff (from left) Wayne Lamb, Hermine Kahlich Kroll, Donald Polk and Ira McCarver (1939). *Courtesy of Slaton Railroad Heritage Association.*

engines were repaired) would deliver coal down a coal shoot into the Harvey House basement: "I had to bring the coal up to the kitchen to fuel the stove. Most people don't know we cooked with coal." And most people don't know that a small steam-powered engine was used to crank the ice cream made fresh daily. This was another of Lamb's duties. The steam was piped from the round house and also heated the Harvey House. "Another job I had was to meet the 7:00 morning train," Lamb said. "I had to wear a white coat and stand out on the platform beside the tracks beating on a gong and yelling, 'Breakfast is being served inside.'" Calvin's brother, Wayne Lamb, also worked as a busboy at the Slaton Harvey House. After high school, Calvin worked for the Santa Fe on the line gang and then joined the navy. He returned to work for the Santa Fe again in the train department, where he remained for forty-one years. He retired in 1987 as a conductor.

Every Harvey House has its own history shaped by the individuals who worked there. Whether fact or fiction, it has been reported that Harvey Girls learned to roller skate in the basement of the Slaton Harvey House and that, at another time, the underground space housed a beer-making operation supervised on the sly by the German chef. Other stories indicate that a Harvey Girl climbing down the trellis from a second-floor window to meet a cowboy was not that uncommon.

The primary purpose of the Harvey House was to feed passengers when the train stopped for service. However, the Slaton Harvey House enjoyed

Current photo of restored Harvey House in Slaton, Texas. *Courtesy of Slaton Railroad Heritage Association.*

the reputation as the finest restaurant in the area. A well-paid (annual salary of up to $5,000) chef prepared meals with deliberate attention to the details outlined by the main office in Kansas City, Missouri. Food was served on plates kept warm in a steamer, and the tables were covered in crisp, white linen. Soup was always on the menu, requiring the chef to prepare fifteen gallons daily. Often, wealthy people drove twenty miles from the larger town of Lubbock to dine, and Slatonites ate there for special occasions.

The Slaton Harvey House closed in 1943, briefly reopening to serve troops who were transported by train during World War II. The building was used by the Santa Fe as a passenger depot until 1969. When the passenger service along this route was discontinued because of a sharp decline in customers, the space was used as a Santa Fe railroad yard office until 1980, when the once vibrant Harvey House was abandoned.

The residents of Slaton saved the Harvey House building from the Santa Fe wrecking ball in 1989. The Slaton Railroad Heritage Association organized to oversee the dream of restoration. In 2007, the Slaton Harvey House opened as a bed-and-breakfast, and there is space to rent for meetings, receptions and other special events.

Brownwood (1914–1938/1940–1944)

The last Texas Harvey House opened in Brownwood, county seat of Brown County, in 1914, at a time when the town was enjoying a growth in population primarily because it had become the Central Texas junction for several railroad lines. Brownwood's population grew from almost four thousand at the beginning of the twentieth century to approximately seven thousand residents ten years later. The design of the tan brick Harvey House building stayed true to Santa Fe buildings of the time, with dark brown trim and a red Spanish tile roof. A covered walkway joined the Harvey facilities to the Santa Fe Depot (built in 1910), giving an effect of one large building. The interior décor of the Harvey House featured stenciling on the walls and ceiling. Door and window frames, wainscoting and plate rails were made of English oak.

H.A. Rutter was sent to Brownwood to oversee the opening of the lunchroom after working eighteen months at the Rosenberg Harvey House. The opening of the dining room was postponed a month because of a delay in the shipping of custom furniture that would seat forty-eight diners.

The *Brownwood Daily Bulletin* reported, "The new Harvey House at the Santa Fe passenger station was opened to the public at 7 o'clock this morning and there was an immediate rush of business." Eighteen Harvey employees greeted the first customers. In the grandiose style of newspaper writing typical of the time, the article declared that "everything that could add to convenience of travelling public has been installed." Describing the Harvey House as

Railroad station and Harvey House in Brownwood, Texas. *Courtesy of ATSFry.com, R.L. Crump Library Collection, Copy and Reuse Restrictions Apply.*

Harvey House dining room in Brownwood, Texas. *Courtesy of ATSFry.com, R.L.Crump Library Collection, Copy and Reuse Restrictions Apply.*

"magnificent," the news story further declares that "an attempt to describe the new Harvey House would be futile because several newspaper columns would not afford space enough to go into details regarding this handsome new building and its magnificent equipment. The kitchen is arranged with a view to accessibility and every appliance known to modern cookery is installed there." It was also reported that the Harvey House cost $50,000 to construct.

A wedding announcement in *Santa Fe Magazine* is one more reminder that through the years, the Harvey rules for employees relaxed. In 1919, Miss Josephine Fowler, "universally known as one of the best newsstand managers on the [Harvey] system," married Earle G. Livingston, manager of the Brownwood House, who began his Harvey career ten years earlier as a cashier in the Topeka, Kansas Harvey House. Apparently, employees were allowed to date and marry, as was documented in this publication distributed throughout the Santa Fe and Fred Harvey system. It seems Miss Fowler was quite a catch. In the article about the wedding, she was described as "always pleasant, agreeable, and smiling."

As passenger travel grew, the Harvey House staff was increased to serve more customers. In 1922, eight years after the Brownwood restaurant opened, there were thirty-six Harvey staff employed.

In the late 1920s, that famous Fred Harvey coffee was a dime a cup, and one of the newer drinks available, Coca-Cola, was also a dime. A slice of pie was twenty-five cents, you could get two doughnuts for five cents, two eggs cost a quarter and pancakes were twenty cents. The cost of the noon lunch was sixty-five cents, and a tenderloin steak was seventy-five cents.

According to Harvey House cook W.T. Powers, Brown County farmers sold fresh fruit and vegetables, pecans and turkeys to the local Harvey House, and in some instances, these products were shipped to other Harvey House locations. He said, "Many turkeys raised in Brown County could be found in the Harvey restaurants around the United States at Thanksgiving and Christmas."

The small room in the Brownwood Harvey House where diners could leave personal items such as coats, scarves and hats contained a small table and chairs. This space was where the black train porters and other employees were served their meals.

In the 1920s, Ruth Norville visited her sister and brother-in-law, Charles and Stella Scott, in Brownwood. The couple worked in both the Cleburne Harvey House and the Brownwood location. Ruth remembered the Brownwood Harvey House as being more elaborate and having a huge dining room where not only train passengers ate, but many local civic clubs as well. She said, "The food was delicious in all of these houses. They had to hold up the trains many times in order for the people to finish eating their delicious meals." Ruth fondly recalled the delicious coffee and pies, "especially coconut custard, and homemade vanilla ice cream."

John Preas, whose wife, Lillian, became a Harvey Girl, began working at the Brownwood Harvey House as a pantry man and later as a baker. This employment situation was unusual because at the time married couples were not allowed to work together at a Harvey House. When I met with Lillian to hear her Harvey Girl story, she explained, "John had worked as a pantry man, and we went to the Harvey House to visit. The manager asked John if he would come back as a baker. John told him there weren't enough pennies to bring him back." Lillian continued with a smile, "Then the manager also offered me a job in the Lunch Room, hoping that would entice John to come back. I had never worked as a waitress, but that was not a problem as the Harvey House preferred to train their staff."

Lillian took the job, and John went to work as the baker. "When I had to follow the head waitress to learn how to do things, I was never so scared in all of my life," Lillian said. "Her name was Gertrude, and she could carry six cups of coffee at one time. Eventually, I got to where I could take five at a time, but it was a while before I could carry six. I never did spill one, though."

"They kept an eye on the waitresses," Lillian continued. "The girls were expected to keep everything clean, spotless and provide perfect service. We didn't visit with the customers. If someone asked you a question, you just answered and went on about your business. It was exciting, though, when the trains came in. We served passengers from all over the United States." In addition to realizing her unusual situation of being married to another Harvey employee, Lillian considered her role of a working wife and mother significant in a time when most married women did not work.

Lillian would go to work early in the morning to serve the first train passengers of the day and then remove her white, starched apron and walk the block to her home, often to do the family laundry under the trees in the front yard. After "rubbing out" the laundry and putting it in rinse water, Lillian returned to the Harvey House again at lunch. Following that shift, she would go home to "wring out" the clothes and put them on the line to dry. When Lillian finished her final shift of the day, she would walk home, bring in the dry clothes, fold them and put them away. She considered this "quite a deal for a married woman!"

The Preas couple worked during the Depression years, and Lillian thought they were "two of the lucky ones." John worked his way up from $75 a month to $125, and Lillian made fifty to seventy-five cents a day. Additionally, the free meals at the Harvey House helped them get through the tough times. The Harvey Girls worked seven days a week until the loss of customers during the Depression forced the manager to offer the women a choice. "We could either each have one day off a week or one of us would be laid off. We all took a day off."

In a letter following my visit with Lillian, she emphasized how pleasant the work atmosphere was at the Harvey House: "Never did we ever hear an ugly word used or never a crass word spoken by anyone. You were treated as a lady or a gentleman at all times."

After the Harvey House closed, John and Lillian Preas owned a restaurant and trained their waitresses in the same way Lillian had been trained. She said, "My time at the Harvey House paid off. It helped me know how to run a restaurant and how to deal with employees." In 1997, the *Brownwood Bulletin* printed a photo of Lillian, age ninety-eight, wearing a duplicate of her Harvey Girl uniform that she had recently made.

The Preases' daughter, Bessie Mae "Bunk" Ellis, provided a child's perspective of life at the Brownwood Harvey House. "We were a happy family. Dad bought a house close to the Harvey House so we kids could walk there after school. I loved going there. Everyone was so nice. The man in the baggage

Dear Rosa,

I to enjoyed your nice visit, and time went so fast. I called my daughter mrs. Ellis, also mrs. Piper and told them what a nice visit we had. Yes! I remember Lucille and Leona I bought two uniforms from them when they left Brownwood— You might use this little in your news, never did we ever hear an ugly word used or never a cross word spoken by any one— You was treated as a Lady or a Gen- tleman at all times— my thoughts will remain with you, You.

Lillian Preas.

Personal letter to author from Brownwood Harvey Girl Lillian Preas. *Author's collection.*

room—we called him 'Candy'—would give us rides on the baggage carts and weigh us on the big scale." Ellis also remembered that the wife of one of the managers would practice her tap dancing upstairs in their apartment: "We could hear her in the dining room." Frequent visits to the depot broadened Bunk's view of the world outside of Brownwood. She remembered, "We loved meeting the trains! I saw a Catholic nun for the first time at the depot, and I also remember seeing Japanese sailors. I'm sure I stared!"

William Fonash, well regarded throughout the Harvey system for his efficiency in training personnel, was manager at Brownwood before moving to the Fort Worth Harvey House Lunch Room. Other Harvey guys at the Brownwood location between 1927 and 1931 were: Pete Byrd, dishwasher; Alvie Hutton, newsstand manager; Cecil Hamm, chef; Brownell Adams, busboy and dishwasher; Homer Rose, night cook; Reyhnold Gruening, dinner chef; Bill Hicks, cashier; and George Belt, busboy.

Brownell Adams began in September 1927 as a dishwasher in the Brownwood Harvey House and lived above the Harvey House in one of fourteen rooms for staff. The manager and his wife lived in an apartment at one end of the hallway, and the other rooms were home to waitresses and other unmarried Harvey House employees. The waitresses were on one side of the hall, and the men on the other side. Adams was reluctant to divulge much information. In a newspaper interview, he said, "There were plenty of stories to go with each of those rooms, but I don't really think I should say anything." When Adams married on December 26, 1931, his Harvey House days were over: "I had to get another job to make a little more money." At the time he quit, Adams was making thirty-five dollars a month.

The Brownwood Harvey House closed in 1938 but reopened in 1940 to serve military personnel at the United States National Guard training camp at Camp Bowie. The Bowie facility was also used to train soldiers during World War II. The Harvey House closed permanently four years later.

Evelyn Adams came to work at the Brownwood Harvey House during this time. She remembered trains carrying U.S. troops and prisoners of war that stopped for meals: "There were so many [that] we had to have several seatings to feed them all. They would call ahead with the numbers so we could have the food ready." Evelyn recalled that the soldiers returning home were very thin and that the German prisoners of war barely spoke at all. "It was hard to make change for the soldiers, we were so rushed. We were open twenty-four hours a day." During these days at the Harvey House, the menus were not as varied, as food choices were dictated by what was available. However, quality of the food served was still a priority. Evelyn remembered working with a French chef sent to Brownwood from Chicago and the high demand for coffee, which kept the busboy very busy.

Evelyn was the head waitress and was responsible for training the staff and keeping track of their hours. "I hired and fired. But I only had to fire one Harvey Girl. She had gotten drunk the night before and didn't come down to work the next morning. That kind of behavior was not allowed," Evelyn explained. "I lived on the second floor of the Harvey House and always felt safe. When it was warm, I didn't close the door to my room. I just pulled a curtain across the opening for privacy." She was paid sixty-five dollars a month, and waitresses made forty-five dollars. "Everything was taken care of, so it was easy to save my money." Although Evelyn couldn't recall the Harvey House manager's name, she vividly remembered his sense of humor. At the end of one Christmas Day, after serving troop trains all day, he told her, "You should be so happy. Think of all the men you've met today!"

Originally, the standard uniform for Brownwood Harvey Girls was a black dress with a Dutch collar, a black bow and a white apron with two

Above, left: Former Brownwood, Texas Harvey Girl Evelyn Adams. At the time this photo was taken during an interview with the author in 2014, Mrs. Adams was ninety years old. *Author's collection.*

Above, right: Re-creation of a Harvey Girl's bedroom and replica of typical Harvey Girl uniform on display on the second floor of the restored depot in Brownwood, Texas. *Author's collection.*

large pockets, black shoes and stockings. Harvey Girl Lillian Preas recalled that the uniforms were subject to inspections by the manager's wife. "The hem of the skirt had to be exactly thirteen inches from the ground." When the Harvey House reopened in 1940, the women wore white dresses with a black bow, and the hemline was boldly shortened to just below the knee. Times had changed!

W.T. Powers was the night shift cook and chief baker at the Brownwood Harvey House when it closed in 1944. "I remember they gave us the chance to transfer. I could have transferred to the Harvey House diner in Canadian, Texas [360 miles north of Brownwood], but that was a little too far from home."

Powers remembered that the cooks wore white jackets and handkerchiefs tied around their necks. Some wore tall chef hats, and trousers were white or black-and-white checked. Mrs. Johnson was the manager during the two years Powers worked at the Brownwood Harvey House. "Our chef, Vernon Pruit of Kansas, was great to all of us," Powers said. "I went to work at 6:00 a.m. every day. It was my duty to have doughnuts and cinnamon twists

Current photo showing the original detailed stenciling on the ceiling and walls of the Harvey House Dining Room in Brownwood, Texas. *Author's collection.*

ready by 10:20 a.m." He recalled that most of the customers sat around a horseshoe marble-topped counter.

The last passenger train left the Brownwood depot in July 1968, twenty-four years after the Harvey House closed. The Brownwood Santa Fe Depot and Harvey House Restaurant and Hotel have been restored and are maintained as part of the Brownwood Transportation Complex. The buildings serve as offices for the Brownwood Chamber of Commerce and Visitors Center, the Convention and Tourism Bureau and the Gordon Wood Hall of Champions Sports Museum.

Chapter 3
FINE DINING AT UNION STATION

HARVEY HOUSES IN THE CITY

O that pretty Harvey girl was good to see,
Her presence and her manner made me glad;
As she heaped things on my plate,
I kept busy thanking Fate
For her deftness and the appetite I had.

I have heard great Paderewski pound the keys,
But the pretty Harvey girl, as I'm a sinner,
Produced the blithest of all melodies
As she clicked the plates while handing me my dinner.
—S.E. Kiser

At the time the first Texas Harvey House eating establishment opened in Galveston's Union Station in 1897, Fred Harvey was operating lunchrooms, dining rooms, newsstands and hotels in eleven other states. Although the surroundings were quite different from Harvey Houses in rural Texas, Harvey Girls, starched linens and quality food greeted passengers in the bustling Union Stations of Galveston, El Paso, Houston, Dallas and Fort Worth. The designation "union station" applied to railroad depots where two or more separate railway companies shared the tracks and facilities. Rural Harvey Houses were in or adjacent to Santa Fe Railroad depots.

Train passengers using several railway companies meant a constant flow of customers in the Union Station Harvey House restaurants. The lunchroom provided fast service and excellent food twenty-four hours a day. Passengers with plenty of time before catching another train enjoyed the fine dining ambiance of the Harvey dining room. The Harvey House dining rooms were also popular for special local events such as bridal luncheons, graduation parties and civic dinners. These occasions were often noted on the "Women's Page" of the local newspaper, with descriptive phrases such as "jovial gathering" and "jolly farewell luncheon."

A typical Union Station menu would offer a "Plate Lunch" for seventy-five cents served weekdays from 11:00 a.m. to 2:30 p.m. A luncheon special cost fifty cents and gave customers a choice of "broiled ham with mushrooms on toast, supreme; fricasse [sic] of lamb, dumplings and peas or beef a la mode, jardinere [sic], potato pancake with a roll, butter" and choice of coffee, tea or milk. A choice of dessert was included: custard pie, loganberry pie, ice cream cake or bread and butter pudding.

A variety of sandwiches were available any time of the day, including a fried egg sandwich for fifteen cents or a minced ham and Swiss cheese on rye with cucumber rings for thirty-five cents. The most exotic sandwich, by Texas standards, might have been fried oysters on toast with cole slaw for thirty-five cents.

A Union Station Harvey House dinner usually cost one dollar and offered a choice of broiled black sea bass, mushroom omelette, grilled lamb chops, broiled sirloin or roasted chicken. The diner also got a first course of tomato juice, consommé or sweet watermelon cubes and, to accompany their entree, a combination salad with French dressing, au gratin potatoes and June peas, along with coffee, tea or milk. This hearty meal was served daily from 5:00 to 9:00 p.m. and from 11:30 a.m. to 8:30 p.m. on Sunday.

Fred Harvey Newsstands offered train passengers an interesting array of newspapers, magazines and books, as well as an excellent selection of cigars. These Harvey businesses often stayed open many years after the restaurants were closed.

As if the desserts displayed under glass domes at the lunch counter were not enough of a temptation, imagine the delight of small travelers when they saw the gleaming Harvey soda fountain serving frothy delights thick with freshly made ice cream. Other Harvey establishments in Texas Union Stations included barbershops, bars and, in El Paso, a "curio" shop called the Indian Room.

Another popular Fred Harvey enterprise in the Union Stations was the Photomatic photo booths. For a few cents, you could pop into a small booth, pull the curtain and pose for a photo. Soon you were rewarded with a small

Top: Johnny Wessels, son of a Harvey House chef, in a photo taken at the Fred Harvey Photomatic photo booth at Union Station in Houston, Texas, circa 1938. *Courtesy of Ann Wessels Bratcher.*

Left: The back of the metal frame for photos taken in the Fred Harvey Photomatic photo booth. *Courtesy of Ann Wessels Bratcher.*

picture in a metal frame with "Fred Harvey Restaurant and Shops" stamped on the back, along with space to personalize the souvenir by writing in your name, the location and date. The photo booth was a novelty of the time, and many couples and families leaving the Harvey House after a fine meal must have stopped to celebrate the special event with a cozy photo.

As the train stations expanded or new ones were built in Houston, Dallas and Fort Worth, the Harvey House history becomes less precise. However, given the dates of operation from Fred Harvey company files, it appears that the Harvey businesses evolved along with these growing centers of commerce and transportation. There were always Harvey Girls in uniform efficiently serving delicious food, and we can be certain that the same Fred Harvey standards were maintained in these urban locations. In addition to the more frequent arrival of trains and much larger numbers of potential customers, perhaps the biggest difference for the women who worked in the Union Station Harvey Houses was that there were no living quarters provided, making Harvey rules regarding their personal lives more difficult to enforce.

Just as a rural Harvey House served as an oasis of civility on the railroad line stretching across Texas, Harvey House restaurants offered respite in the noisy, crowded Union Stations in large cities where many railroad lines converged. Travelers of all kinds found a consistent refuge in the hands of dedicated, well-trained Harvey Girls and the values of the Harvey way.

The exemplary service at the El Paso Harvey House was praised in a letter from "A Unit of Nurses" dated April 20, 1946. The letter was sent to the Fred Harvey corporate headquarters in Chicago and found its way to the desk of Byron Harvey Sr., Fred Harvey's younger son and president of the company at that time.

> *Dear Sir: For a long time I have intended to write to you. Seeing the picture* The Harvey Girls *made me know more than ever I must write. The advertisement in* Fortune *magazine showing the Syracuse china made us appreciate the dishes our food was served from. Not a chipped or cracked one on the table.*
>
> *In our travels we were transferred to El Paso, Texas. It was between eleven and twelve at night when we arrived at the station. Several of us went into the dining room; after days of traveling in hot coaches and having only two meals, we were so pleased to be in a cool room, where everyone was so pleasant.*
>
> *The most courteous and sweet gray-haired lady took our order. We all noticed the efficient way she served her customers. All agreed someone should*

write and thank her. Through you we want to tell her that we will never forget the person that showed us how to be gracious.

[signed] *A Unit of Nurses.*

Byron Harvey Sr. distributed a copy of the letter to "All Fred Harvey Managers" with this attached note:

Gentlemen: I give below a letter which, while fairly similar to others, is especially interesting for the following reasons: (1) Since the letter is anonymous, the senders could not hope to gain anything by writing it. (2) It indicates that the motion picture The Harvey Girls *did have some effect on the people who saw it. (3) It proves that advertising, in certain instances at least, has value especially when it is backed up by courteous service. (4) It proves how important thoughtful courtesy is on the part of people serving the traveling public and that attention to detail such as the elimination of cracked chinaware, is noticed and appreciated. If you think well of the idea and have a suitable place to do so, I suggest that you post this letter on your bulletin board. Yours very truly,* [signed] *Byron Harvey, Sr.*

Fred Harvey's original plan was to provide a place for passengers to eat approximately every one hundred miles when the trains stopped for fuel. In later years, the choice of Texas Harvey House locations was most likely influenced by other factors. We do know, however, that not every town that wanted a Harvey House got one. A letter to Fred Harvey from the president of the Stamford Town Site Company, Charles Hamilton, dated November 6, 1900, described a "very nice and complete little hotel" furnished "throughout with the nicest kind of furniture and fixtures. The building will be supplied with water, steam heat and electric lights and should be ready for occupancy by the first of December." Mr. Hamilton explained that "we want this hotel managed better than any other hotel in Texas and this is to ask if you would consider the question. If not, could you recommend a first-rate hotel manager, married man preferred?" We don't have Mr. Harvey's response, but we know that there was no Harvey House in Stamford, Texas.

Another letter to Mr. Harvey, dated April 1, 1905, is from a representative of the Southwest Development Association in Houston proposing a Harvey Hotel "practically on the top of the Galveston sea wall." Mr. Dickensheets assured Harvey that "a hotel built here would be seventeen feet above the sea, fine lawns, splendid boulevard thirty miles in length capital for automobiling, etc." He promised, "The Southwest Development Association is willing to undertake floating the stock, providing it could get someone like you to manage the hotel and take an interest." Galveston was the site of the first Harvey House restaurant in Texas; however, there was never a Harvey Hotel atop the sea wall.

GALVESTON (1897–1938)

Union Station in Galveston, Texas, circa 1897. *Courtesy of Michael McMillan.*

The Galveston Harvey House Lunch Room and Newsstand operated in the original, red brick train station until 1914, when both were moved to the new, expansive Union Station. The art-deco building featured bold geometric shapes and lavish ornamentation. The lunch counter seated thirty-four diners and, as with all Harvey Houses, was a favorite eating spot for locals as well as train passengers. However, in this coastal city, it was also a favorite of passengers on the steam liners that docked nearby. Some of these travelers would come ashore simply to enjoy a good meal, and others would leave the ship, stop for a meal and then board a train for their final destination.

Galveston Harvey Girl Mary Magdalene (Madge) Jones worked in the Harvey Lunch Room from 1935 to 1938. She said, "A friend told me they needed a waitress. Two girls applied: she had experience and I didn't." Madge had just graduated from high school in Baird, Texas (approximately four hundred miles northwest of Galveston) and wondered why she was

Hand-tinted postcard of the interior of the original Galveston Union Station. *Courtesy of Michael McMillan.*

chosen for the job, especially after her comment during the interview that she would be "like a donkey in a china store." She later learned the Fred Harvey company preferred to train the Harvey Girls. After two weeks of training, she made "forty dollars a month for ten hours a day, six days a week, meals and laundry and usually three dollars to three-and-a-half dollars a week tips. That went in my savings account.

"It was a job you were trained to do right. For that was a hallmark of Fred Harvey restaurants throughout the United States." Madge remembered that meals included soup, salad and a "regular course" dinner with steak, lamb chops, fish or chicken. "The salads were not tossed salad like they serve today. We served pear or pineapple with cottage cheese; sliced tomatoes; a Waldorf salad or a wedge of lettuce with the best dressing." Meals cost from sixty-five cents to eighty-five cents for lunch and one dollar and eighty-five cents for dinner, although "some meals cost a little more." The rolls, salad dressing and "hand-cranked" ice cream were made fresh in the Harvey House kitchen. She said, "We got our meat, milk, butter and eggs out of Kansas City every morning on the Santa Fe."

Menus were also sent throughout the Harvey system from the main office in Kansas City, Missouri, which helped uphold a quality of food service that is still considered unique to Fred Harvey restaurants. Additionally, a

Left: Mary Magdalene (Madge) Jones Saenz, Harvey Girl in the Galveston Union Station Harvey House, 1935–38. *Courtesy of Raymond Saenz.*

Below: Harvey Girls with the Harvey House manager behind the lunch counter in Union Station, Galveston, Texas. *Courtesy of Raymond Saenz.*

rotation of entrees and special dishes ensured that passengers traveling for several days could enjoy a variety of meals. If menu items were not available locally to maintain the company-dictated meal plan, food products were shipped, on ice if necessary. Using this system, a Harvey Girl could serve fresh mountain trout to a patron in landlocked Slaton, Texas. The use of the Santa Fe Railroad, at no charge, by the Fred Harvey company to ship food, supplies and laundry was part of the original hand-shake agreement between the railway company and Mr. Harvey in 1876.

"On Sunday morning we had to polish all the silver, which included silverware, teapots, sugar bowls, cake stands and coffee pots," Madge wrote. "We had to change our uniform from black and white, black shoes and hose to all white uniform only on Sundays. The place setting had to be right, and we served from right to left. We had big crowds on the weekend.

"We also served breakfast to the Mallory Steamship Line passengers, who boarded the steamers at Twenty-fifth Street," Madge said. "Many left a silver dime tip." However, she added, "Railroad employees did not always leave a tip." She recalled that breakfast usually included waffles with bacon and a horseshoe cut of ham. She added, "We also served apple pie and good coffee."

Serving celebrities and other notables of the time was not uncommon for a Harvey Girl. Madge remembered serving entertainer Phil Harris in the Galveston Harvey House: "Later he married Alice Faye at the Galvez Hotel. I also served President Franklin D. Roosevelt when he came to go deep sea fishing in the Gulf [of Mexico], and he boarded his private rail car in the train station."

After working six months, Madge asked to use the train pass she had earned to go home for a visit: "I was so homesick. I rode to Fort Worth on the pass and paid my way from Fort Worth to Baird. I stopped in Dallas for the State Fair and didn't have a room reservation." She asked a policeman if he knew where she might get a room and "he sent me to his home." Her good fortune didn't end there. "I won a Southwestern Bell Telephone call at the fair and called my nephew at school because we didn't have a phone at home."

Madge Jones recalled the employees who were working with her at the time this Harvey location closed in 1938: waitresses Anna Dixon, Marie Olsen, Mabel Eubanks, Emma Lee and Lydia Quinn; cooks Elbert and Delbert Pittman; busboys Joe Campo, Johnny Scrofine, Sam Bell and Tommy Melertin; and pantry girl Phoebe Pleasant. Joe Campo began working at the Galveston Harvey House in 1914 and remained an employee there until it closed.

When the restaurant closed, employees were given the opportunity to transfer to any of the other Harvey Houses, but Madge chose to stay in Galveston. "I had just married and bought furniture. I wasn't going

Galveston Harvey Girls (from left) Marie Olsen, Madge Saenz and Lydia Quinn. The trio worked together beginning in the mid-1930s until the Harvey House closed in 1938. *Courtesy of Raymond Saenz.*

to give that up. I was so proud to be a Harvey Girl and wear the uniforms," she reminisced. "We did look nice and the place was so quiet and beautiful!"

The Galveston Harvey House reopened in 1942 to serve the World War II soldiers who arrived on the train. Some Harvey employees came back to help, but Madge Jones Saenz was, by then, working full time at the Star Drug Store.

Some of the Harvey guys who managed the Galveston Harvey House include Robert Otis Thomas (1930–32 and 1934–35) and J.A. Klug (1936–37). When the Galveston Lunch Room closed, Manager L.K. Cox transferred to the LaFonda Hotel in Santa Fe, New Mexico, which was also owned by Fred Harvey. Ray Razey is listed in Fred Harvey records as manager of the newsstand in Galveston's Union Station (1945–46). The newsstand remained in business until April 11, 1967, when the last passenger train left Galveston. The highly rated Galveston Railroad Museum is now located in the Union Station structure.

Madge Jones Saenz returned to work as a Harvey Girl in 1986 when a restaurant was established in dining cars at the Railroad Museum located in the Union Passenger Station. She made a replica of one of her original uniforms and worked on the weekends seating guests and telling her Harvey Girl story. "I didn't know that being a Harvey House Girl would mean so much to me," Saenz said. "I was thrilled to get to work four more years as a Harvey Girl again."

DALLAS (1901–1923)

The Dallas Harvey House lunchroom, dining room and newsstand began operations in 1901 in the Santa Fe depot. The Harvey businesses transitioned into the new Union Station built in1916. Considered the state's first rail crossroads, the new station was designed to handle fifty thousand passengers daily, traveling on as many as eighty trains.

The Fred Harvey organization was up for the challenge. For many years, the Fred Harvey company was profitable in spite of the generous portions of food, the low prices and elaborate surroundings. Mr. Harvey's original agreement with the Santa Fe Railroad served the company well for many years. In addition to the railroad providing supplies such as coal, water and ice free of charge, the Harvey company did not pay rent for space occupied by its businesses. Decline in profits and eventual closing of many locations were brought about by increased automobile travel and the successful addition of dining cars on passenger trains.

The service and quality of food found in all Harvey Houses was well known; however, the coffee had a reputation all its own. From the very beginning, Fred Harvey stressed the quality of the coffee and established strict rules dictating that it be freshly brewed every two hours. The blend of Harvey House coffee was adjusted for local water to maintain consistent quality. If the local water was deemed unsuitable, water was brought in by train. Train travel during this time could be grueling, with no heat in the winter and no way to stay cool in the summer. Seating was uncomfortable, and dust mingled with soot permeated the passenger cars. The simple pleasure of a fresh, hot cup of good coffee was surely a welcome experience for many travelers.

A Fred Harvey company brochure circa 1905 touted the quality of food served along the Santa Fe, including the Union Station dining rooms. "The steaks are thick, juicy and tender. The cream is the genuine article. The fruits are always seasonable. The menu is varied and satisfying because Harvey's chefs have the food products of a continent at their command. The service is perfect." The printed piece further entices the train passenger: "The conductor does not cry 'all aboard!' just when you are half way [*sic*] through the bill of fare. He waits until the last passenger has finished."

The last privately owned passenger train left the Dallas Union Station in 1969, and two years later, Amtrak began passenger service. The building was renovated in 2008, and now Amtrak, Trinity Railway Express and Dallas Area Rapid Transit stations occupy the first floor. The second floor

Union Terminal in Dallas, Texas. *Courtesy of Michael McMillan.*

The Harvey House Dining Room in Union Station, Dallas, Texas. *Courtesy of Special Collections/University of Arizona Library/Fred Harvey: Traveling the Rails in Grand Style collection.*

houses space that can be rented for meetings and private parties. It should be noted that all events at the historic Union Station are catered exclusively by Wolfgang Puck Catering. I think Fred Harvey would approve!

EL PASO (1906–1948)

The opening of the first international train station in the United States, the El Paso Union Depot, on February 27, 1906, was a celebrated event for the city of thirty-five thousand. The facility was described as being built of Texas brick and Texas lumber with El Paso labor and contractor. The *El Paso Times* reported that over ten thousand attended the reception and dance on opening night. "Only persons whose conduct would not warrant their admission" were excluded from attending the affair. Anticipated attractions of the new depot were the Harvey House dining room and lunch counter, as well as a Harvey-operated bar, barbershop, newsstand and gift shop. However, the *Evening News* warned readers that the "Harvey furniture is not here. The dining room, and the news stand will be fitted with special furniture made to order and this has not arrived." John Stein, superintendent of the Harvey company lunchrooms headquartered in Las Vegas, New Mexico, was quoted regarding the delay: "It takes time to construct the fixtures for the lunchroom. The marble topped lunch counter

Current photo of the bell tower of the Union Station building in El Paso, Texas. *Author's collection.*

These stately oak doors and intricate tile floor design once marked the entrance to the Fred Harvey bar in Union Station, El Paso, Texas. *Author's collection.*

and the display stand for the lunch counter require time for construction. They could not be hastily thrown together."

The newspaper also reported that "the sign painter has just finished his task, and in letters of gold, the public is made aware of the situation: 'Ticket Office,' 'Smoking Room,' 'Colored Waiting Room' and similar signs greet the visitor on every side."

Almost a month after the official opening of Union Station, the Harvey newsstand opened under makeshift conditions. A news story reported, "The fittings of this department have not yet been completed"; however, "demands of travelers for souvenir postal cards are being satisfied." Once the "fittings" for the newsstand were complete and the merchandise was in place, train passengers were met with an assortment of newspapers, magazines, candy, cigars and cigarettes. A large placard showing a classy young lady with two wolfhounds advertised Old Gold Cigarettes with the slogan "America's Smoothest Cigarettes. Not a Cough in a Carload."

Dozens of magazines such as *Popular Mechanic*, *Harper's Bazaar* and *Cosmopolitan* were prominently displayed, along with a variety of popular newspapers from large U.S. cities. Small, colorful cactus plants were sold as local souvenirs.

On April 25, 1906, train passengers and El Pasoans alike could enjoy the much-anticipated service and food at the Harvey House in Union Station. Less than two weeks before, it was reported that "three girls who will be employed in the Harvey Eating room at the new Union Station have arrived." No doubt these were experienced Harvey Girls sent to train the new staff in El Paso. The *El Paso Herald* quite eloquently described the dining room as having "walls of fumed oak paneling to a height of seven feet, with a finish approximating in effect weathered leather of a deep tan shade. Every detail is carried out perfectly. Electric table lamps with art glass shades add greatly to the effect." The adjacent lunch counter, open "24 hours out of each day," had "comfortable revolving chairs" and "heavy fumed oak and marble counters."

Practical aspects of the Harvey House operation were also covered in detail by the newspaper: "Perhaps the most interesting part of the Harvey concession is the system of storage closets, refrigerating compartments and the kitchen equipment. The refrigerators all are lined with white enamel, assuring the high degree of cleanliness and sanitary conditions." Stating the Harvey policy, "First get the right materials and then prepare them right," the *Herald* reporter added, "This policy is carried out regardless of expense or inconvenience."

Once the Harvey House was open, the quality of food and service most certainly met that well-known Harvey standard. However, train passengers familiar with Harvey Houses along the Santa Fe would notice one difference at this site. The El Paso Harvey House staff was more ethnically diverse than most Harvey establishments because of the large Hispanic population who lived there.

According to El Paso Harvey Girl Lillian Mendez, her uniform was a variation of those worn by Harvey Girls throughout the system: white skirt to the knee, white blouse, black bow tie, white shoes and stockings. Bertha Mendez, who was a busgirl in the 1940s, recalled that her uniform was a white shirt, brown pants and brown shoes. "We had to wear a clean uniform every day," she added.

Jose Ornales was a salad boy at the El Paso Harvey House, also during the 1940s. He later transferred to another Harvey House, the Bright Angel Lodge in the Grand Canyon, and, after several years, returned to El Paso, where he opened two successful restaurants. "I learned everything about the restaurant business from being a Fred Harvey employee," Ornelas recalled.

The El Paso Harvey businesses were not staffed entirely with local residents. One example was related to me by the granddaughter of Harvey Girl Kelpie Ann Rainey. "I think my grandmother just wanted to go somewhere exciting and get away from home," Jacky Slaughter explained. Slaughter's grandmother grew up in the tiny town of Vanderpool, Texas, and somehow learned about openings for Harvey Girls in El Paso, five hundred miles west of her hometown. Slaughter said, "I don't know how

Group photo of Fred Harvey company employees at Union Station, El Paso, Texas. *Courtesy of Northern Arizona University, Cline Library, Fred Harvey Collection.*

Lillian Mendez Medina, a 1944 Harvey Girl at Union Station in El Paso. This photo was taken in 2012 at the 106th anniversary of the opening of the depot and Fred Harvey businesses in El Paso, Texas. *Courtesy of Harvey Girls of El Paso.*

Jose Ornales, former salad boy for the El Paso, Texas Harvey House, is pictured with Prestene Dehrkoop in 2012. *Courtesy of Harvey Girls of El Paso.*

she made the arrangements, but my grandmother knew she had a job in El Paso and caught a ride with a couple who was driving through there on their way to California." Kelpie Ann worked a few years as a Harvey Girl in El Paso and then married a railroad engineer.

In a 1940 letter addressed to *Reader's Digest* in response to an article printed about Harvey Houses, former Harvey Girl Gertrude K. Burton, originally from Ireland, told about transferring from Chicago in 1898 to a Las Vegas, New Mexico Harvey establishment and then to the Harvey House in Union Station, El Paso, where she spent the last fifteen years with the Harvey system. Gertrude recalled serving five governors at one table, one of which was the governor of Chihuahua, Mexico. She also served General Pershing in El Paso and on another occasion was sent from El Paso to Deming, New Mexico, to serve then secretary of the navy Franklin D. Roosevelt. Further describing her years in El Paso, Gertrude said, "How often have I stood at the Harvey House window, watching the changes in old Mount Franklin! The sunsets there were beyond description. I thought no other place could be so lovely."

"Harvey Girls of El Paso" is a very active group of women dedicated to keeping the Harvey Girl story alive in the area. The group meets regularly and sponsors

Interior of the Union Station building in El Paso, Texas. Original tile floors, stained-glass accents and other architectural features were preserved in a 1980s restoration. *Author's collection.*

special events, such as a reception in 2012 marking the 106th anniversary of the opening of the Harvey House that brought Harvey Girls to the city.

The Union Station depot was restored in the 1980s. An Amtrak station serves passengers in the original main waiting room. Space once bustling with Harvey hospitality—the bar, dining room and lunch counter—is now used for Texas Tech University School of Architecture offices. The space has been well preserved, and visitors can still experience the opulence and dignity of the depot through the original tile floors with intricate borders, the stained-glass detail in doors once leading to the Harvey House and the ornate second-floor balustrade.

Houston (1911–1948)

The Houston Harvey House operations included a lunchroom and newsstand in Union Station. Both opened when the new station began receiving passengers in 1911 and closed in 1948.

Ann Wessels Bratcher remembers as a child leaving the Enunciation Catholic Church in downtown Houston and crossing the intersection of Texas and Crawford with her mother, sister and brother. This was their

Above: Union Station in Houston, Texas. *Courtesy of Michael McMillan.*

Left: Chef John Wessels with his daughter, Mary Louise. Wessels was chef at the Harvey House, Union Station in Houston, Texas, until he transferred to the Deming, New Mexico Harvey House. *Courtesy of Ann Wessels Bratcher.*

Hand-tinted postcard of the interior of the original Union Station in Houston, Texas. *Courtesy of Michael McMillan.*

weekly visit to Union Station to have lunch at the Harvey House Lunch Room, where her father, John Wessels, was the chef. Ann said, "I can still remember the smell of the luggage, piled on carts being pushed through the depot. The ceilings were so tall, and there were big columns." Ann's mother, Zadie, worked as a Harvey Girl at the Houston restaurant, met John and they were soon married. "Mother didn't work as a Harvey Girl after they married. She stayed home." John Wessels was later transferred to the Deming, New Mexico Harvey House. "I think they were having some problems there, and my dad was sent to straighten things out," Ann explained.

Harvey Girl Ruth Norville, who worked for a short time in the Houston Harvey House, described it as "beautiful," with a counter in the center of the room and, as was typical in all Harvey Houses, beautiful white tablecloths with settings of polished silver and crisp white napkins. "It was a favorite place to eat for many prominent people who worked at the many businesses around Union Station. I can still hear them calling the trains when they were departing for different places. Those were the days. I treasure the fond memories!"

The last train to serve the Houston Union Station was in 1974. The restored building is now the main entrance to Minute Maid Park, home of the Houston Astros major-league baseball team.

FORT WORTH (1913–1933)

Unlike the Harvey House eating establishments in other Texas Union Stations, the Fort Worth dining room, lunchroom and newsstand were in a separate, small building wedged trackside between the passenger and freight

Santa Fe Station and Harvey House in Fort Worth, Texas. *Courtesy of Michael McMillan.*

This Harvey House kitchen in Fort Worth, Texas, is typical of the food preparation equipment and space in all Fred Harvey eating establishments. *Courtesy of Special Collections/University of Arizona Library/Fred Harvey: Traveling the Rails in Grand Style collection.*

depots. The rather plain exterior gave no hint of what awaited customers inside. The paneled dining room and marble-topped lunch counter were in keeping with the "Harvey way" of providing the best in food service in the finest surroundings.

William Fonash, in a 1919 edition of *Santa Fe Magazine*, was commended for being the oldest manager in the Fred Harvey system, having worked for the company for eighteen years. When the "up-to-date eating house" in Fort Worth opened, William was put in charge. Later, he was transferred to the Union Station Harvey House in Galveston. Fonash had the distinction of having taught more cashiers and managers than anyone "on the line" and was known as "Teacher of Managers" for years.

The date the Fort Worth Harvey House was torn down is unknown. The space where the building stood is now a small parking lot.

Chapter 4
SOUVENIRS AND FLAT FIFTIES

HARVEY NEWSSTANDS

*There wasn't a square meal or decent lodging West of St. Louis. There are no
ladies west of Dodge City and no women west of Albuquerque.*
—*Fred Harvey's description of land west of the Mississippi*

In a sense, Fred Harvey newsstands were the twentieth-century forerunner
of modern-day convenience stores. In most Texas Harvey House locations,
the newsstand was inside the Harvey Lunch Room; however, in larger train
depots, it was usually a separate shop that opened into the waiting room
and onto the platform beside the train tracks. The amount and variety of
merchandise offered was in proportion to the number of passengers passing
through the train station.

The first Fred Harvey business in Texas was a newsstand that opened in
the Paris train depot in 1896 and operated until 1930. There was no Harvey
House at this location; however, just thirty miles north in Hugo, Oklahoma,
there was a Harvey House Lunch Room along with a newsstand. The brick
Prairie-style Paris depot has been restored and is used by the Paris Visitors
and Convention Council, Lamar County Genealogical Society, Paris
Economic Development Corporation and Valley of the Caddo Museum.

One other Texas location, Beaumont, had only a Harvey Newsstand and no
eating facility. It is the only Harvey business in Texas that was associated with a
hotel not owned by the Fred Harvey company. The newsstand is listed in a 1905
promotional booklet titled *Fred Harvey Meals* as being located in Beaumont's new
Crosby Hotel. The five-story brick Crosby Hotel was built after the Spindletop

Trackside view of the Paris, Texas Union Station, also known as "Santa Fe–Frisco Depot." A Harvey newsstand inside the depot was the first Fred Harvey business in Texas. *Courtesy of Michael McMillan.*

oil boom of 1901. During that year, the population of Beaumont grew from nine thousand to thirty thousand, and the oil field produced 100,000 barrels of oil a day. The following year, production dropped to 10,000 barrels a day, but the event had changed the economic foundation of Texas.

The oil boom changed the lives of many Texas families as well. One famous example is the subject of the biography *Hughes: The Private Diaries, Memos and Letters.* Author Richard Hack relates that after the Spindletop boom, Howard Hughes Sr. went to Beaumont and "blindly speculated on oil leases from a makeshift office he established at the Crosby Hotel." Hughes eventually established Hughes Tool Company, and after his death in 1924, his son Howard Hughes Jr. inherited the business, parlaying it into a massively successful business conglomerate that made him one of the wealthiest men in the world.

The Crosby Hotel was crowded with men frantically competing to take advantage of the great Texas oil boom. One can only imagine the burgeoning business enjoyed by a Fred Harvey Newsstand, with its sophisticated stock of cigars, cigarettes and current newspapers brought in by train from such faraway cities as Chicago and Kansas City.

Cigarettes and cigars were the prominent merchandise in every Fred Harvey Newsstand. Large Lucky Strike posters featuring young beauties in shorts and ballet slippers declared, "It's toasted!" and "Lucky's are always kind to your throat!" Colorful advertising touted such products as "flat fifties," thin, square tin boxes containing fifty cigarettes popular in the 1940s. The American Tobacco Company included this message inside the tins: "These LUCKY STRIKE CIGARETTES will commend themselves to your critical approval. The additional 'toasting process' adds to the character and improves the taste of the fine tobacco." The Fred Harvey private brand of cigars as well as Roi-Tan, Cremo and Prodigo were sold with the promise, "We give discount on cigars bought by the box."

Chewing gum and candy were also big sellers, and the newsstands were always framed with wire displays of postcards. The postcard business flourished after 1904 when Ford Harvey began working with the Detroit Publishing Company, which had developed a process for colorizing black-and-white photos. A good number of the postcards from the early Harvey days have survived and are often offered online. Many of the images in this book were digitized from original Harvey postcards from the private collection of Michael McMillan, Harvey House historian.

Souvenirs were attractively displayed to appeal to train passengers. Key chains and letter openers, as well as figurines and toy trucks, all clamored for the travelers' attention. Displayed on glass shelves, small items were advertised as souvenirs for bridge prizes. The variety of merchandise was endless: cloisonné compacts, sewing notions, watches and brightly colored felt triangular pennants emblazoned with the state's name.

Solutions for the wide-ranging needs of a traveler were for sale at larger Harvey newsstands. These were listed alphabetically on multi-sided signs with the invitation to ask for articles not listed. Some of those items relieved a traveler's ills: Bromo Quinine cold tablets, Bromo Seltzer for the tummy, liniments, Listerine, Mentholatum and Lavoris. Men's garters and collar buttons were available, as well as cold cream, face powder, Kotex, nail files and perfume for the ladies. Perhaps the most useful remedy available at the newsstands was tins of Cascaret. The advertising for these brown octagonal tablets—reputed to have a taste almost as pleasant as chocolate—promised to eliminate "Heartburn, Colic, Coated Tongue, Suspected Breath, Acid-rising-in-throat, Gas-belching, or an incipient Cold."

Fred Harvey newsstands were a very successful business, and throughout the Harvey system, many survived long after lunchrooms and dining rooms had closed.

The Fred Harvey company broadened the scope of the Harvey Newsstand in the Union Station at El Paso by establishing a separate shop called the Indian

Newsstands were a very successful part of the Fred Harvey company. The one shown was inside the depot in Paris, Texas. *Courtesy of Special Collections/University of Arizona Library/Fred Harvey: Traveling the Rails in Grand Style collection.*

Room. This was in essence a curio shop, but instead of glass figurines and cedar boxes with "El Paso, Texas" stamped on the top, the Indian Room offered authentic Indian artifacts. It appears to have been the only such shop in Texas.

The idea for a commercial partnership between the Fred Harvey company and Indians of the Southwest began when Fred Harvey, who was continually looking for ways to grow his business, observed the Indians gathered to sell handmade items wherever trains stopped in the Southwest. Mr. Harvey noted that passengers, especially from the East, enjoyed shopping with the Indians, an experience that often involved animated negotiating before a final price was reached.

The Harvey company had some experience with Indian merchandise when Harvey employee Herman Schweizer commissioned silver Indian jewelry to sell in some Fred Harvey shops. Fred Harvey could see a greater potential and turned to Minnesota architect Mary Colter for help. He proposed that Colter design an Indian Building as part of the new Harvey hotel in Albuquerque,

New Mexico, called the Alvarado. This was the beginning of a forty-year Colter/Harvey partnership during which she was the designer and decorator of many buildings, including El Tovar, Bright Angel Lodge, Hopi House, Hermit's Rest, Phantom Ranch and Watchtower, all still standing at the Grand Canyon. Mary Colter cultivated a trust with the Indians and was the first to use genuine Southwestern art in interior decorating.

The Alvarado Hotel in Albuquerque opened the year after Fred Harvey's death. The hotel's Indian Building, with its impressive display of American Indian and Eskimo arts and crafts, was very successful. Colter's sense of design in displaying the pottery, baskets and blankets made the merchandise especially appealing. The concept of the Indian Building was translated on a smaller scale into the Indian Room in Union Station, El Paso, offering authentic Indian art to travelers in the far west Texas city.

Chapter 5

UNCERTAIN STOPS

LOST HARVEY HOUSES

Following is a list of Texas towns that are occasionally noted as having been Harvey House locations. In most cases, conclusive documentation has not been found. There are two entries on a list of Fred Harvey operations found in the Fred Harvey Collection, Cline Library, University of Northern Arizona (UNA) that *could* include these locations, although there are no individual towns listed. One entry, with a date of 1883, notes that in that year, "Fred Harvey took over existing eating houses, ATSF, [from] Topeka, [Kansas] to El Paso, [Texas]." Another entry dated 1896 has the notation that Fred Harvey took over existing Frisco eating houses and newsstands, which were located in Missouri, Arkansas, Oklahoma, Tennessee and Texas. All of these establishments were closed by 1930, except in St. Louis, Missouri. This information hints of the possibility that some Texas locations were part of the early Harvey days but for some reason did not survive.

Ray Barbour, a Harvey company manager, added a note addressed to Fred Harvey's grandson Daggett Harvey to a compiled listing of Fred Harvey locations. This list was also found in the UNA archives. The note states: "Please understand this list, to my knowledge, is not completely factual or accurate. I copied from Miss Gerard's data to satisfy my curiosity as to the total number of operations Fred Harvey had acquired at one time or another." The list is titled: "Fred Harvey Hotels—Eating Houses and Newsstands. Copied from a list prepared by Miss Gerard, Chicago Office, April 19th, 1949."

None of the Texas locations discussed in this chapter were on Miss Gerard's list, nor were any mentioned as a Harvey House site in my conversations and

Casa Ricardo Hotel in Kingsville, Texas, on the St. Louis, Brownsville and Mexico Railroad line may have been the site of a Harvey House. *Author's collection.*

correspondence during the research for this book. As Michael McMillan, an individual very knowledgeable about Harvey House history, stated in an e-mail, perhaps in these towns there were places to eat at the depot, and "Harvey House" was used locally in the generic sense, like "Coke" instead soda or "Kleenex" instead of tissue.

Nonetheless, a book about Texas Harvey Houses would not be complete without mentioning these possible Harvey House locations. All of these except Kingsville are listed without photos on the website www.harveyhouses.net.

Bovina: closed 1904
Goldthwaite: no dates available
Kingsville: opened 1912
Ladonia: opened 1887
Lometa: opened 1893
Milano: opened 1889
Navasota: opened 1887
Panhandle: opened 1899
Valley Mills: opened 1888

An online forum commented that a history book of the area was found at the Mills County Museum in Goldthwaite, Texas, with a reference indicating there was a Harvey House there for nine years. However, the title of the book was not available. There is also mention of the Bovina Harvey House on the website http://www.atsfrr.net, stating that before the Harvey House closed in 1904, trains stopped for meals at Bovina.

Though not included on any available inventory listings of Harvey Houses that I found, there is supporting documentation indicating that there was a Harvey House in the Casa Ricardo Hotel in Kingsville, Texas.

The Fred Harvey Company collection at the Heard Museum in Phoenix, Arizona, contains an item titled "Casa Guertrudis, Kingsville, Texas." The Louis Singleton Curtiss collection at the University of Kansas Library (Curtiss, Louis Singleton 1865–1924 Photographs) lists renderings of Casa Guertrudis, Kingsville, Texas, dated 1911, as well as photographs of Casa Ricardo and Frisco Hotel, Kingsville, Texas, dated November 1911. Another entry is a photograph of "Casa Ricardo, Frisco Hotel, a tourist hotel for Frisco RR, Fred Harvey Management." It appears Casa Guertrudis was the proposed name of the establishment, which was later changed to Casa Ricardo.

An application to the United States Department of the Interior, National Park Service, applying for a National Register of Historic Places, also documents the connection between Kingsville and a Fred Harvey establishment: "In 1911–1912, Kansas City architect Louis S. Curtiss undertook a number of projects for the St. Louis, Brownsville and Mexico Railroad in the new town of Kingsville, Texas. One of these was for a tourist hotel called the Casa Ricardo, to be operated under Fred Harvey management. An L-shaped structure with broad eaves and continuous balconies along the interior of the L, the design was one of Curtiss' finest." The entire application is available at http://kcmodern.blogspot.com.

Louis S. Curtiss also designed Texas Santa Fe depots in Post, Snyder, Sweetwater and Lubbock. (Post and Snyder are the only buildings still standing.) He also designed the "boutique" Harvey hotel, El Ortiz in Lamy, New Mexico, as well as the soda fountain and newsstand in Union Station, Wichita, Kansas, and the Bisonte Hotel and Fred Harvey House in Hutchinson, Kansas.

EPILOGUE

O h, the winsome Harvey Girl! We can all learn from your example of courage and character. You thought you were just seeking a more exciting life or increasing your chances for marriage. You accomplished those things, and while you were at it, you created an enduring legacy. A century has passed, and we are still listening to and telling Harvey Girl stories.

Almost every former Harvey employee I spoke with while working on this book began our first conversation with the statement that they didn't really have much to tell. These men and women felt they had just done a job, in the Harvey way, of course, and couldn't conceive that anyone would be interested in their stories. It was fun to hear the energy in their voice as they told of vying for the attention of a certain diner when the manager wasn't watching or innocent pranks they played on the notoriously grumpy chefs. (In defense of those chefs, did you read the recipes in Appendix I? Consider following those vague instructions and cooking on a stove fueled with coal with forty or more hungry train passengers headed to your Harvey House. You would be grumpy, too.)

Working at a Harvey House was often described as being part of a family. In many ways, employees were a nurturing, extended support group. However, I'm sure, as with all families, there were difficult times when envy and suspicion overshadowed relationships. Many Harvey Girls left home for the first time to work in a Harvey House. Of the women I communicated with, only Galveston Harvey Girl Madge Saenz spoke about being homesick. Yet you know at the end of a twelve-hour shift, bone tired and alone on the second floor of the Harvey House, many of these young women cried themselves to sleep.

When Fred Harvey hand-picked waitresses, dressed them in proper, starched uniforms and sent them out to feed the traveling public, I am not sure he realized how Harvey Girls would change the course of women's history. Many were the first to venture more than walking distance from their hometown. Most were the first women in their family to work and to take on a role other than wife and mother. Parents, especially mothers, didn't understand why their daughters chose this strange, perhaps dangerous, new path. Harvey Girls earned wages for the first time in their lives, allowing them to save for an even brighter future or send money home to help a family struggling through the Depression. The attitude back home probably became more anxious when, after six months or a year, those parents received a letter announcing marriage to a Santa Fe brakeman or a local rancher.

Real Harvey Girls didn't sing and dance as much as Judy Garland did in the 1946 movie, but they worked hard, had some fun along the way and made Fred Harvey proud. All these decades later, we are proud and thankful that thousands of women took a path away from familiarity and made life better for everyone in small towns across Texas.

Appendix 1
FROM THE HARVEY HOUSE KITCHENS

Harvey House recipes and kitchen tips featured in the Santa Fe Employes' [sic] Magazine, *in Harvey Service column, 1910–12*

FRIED GREEN TOMATOES

Cut into thin slices some large, perfectly green specimens (they must not have begun to show any sign of ripening, and those freshly pulled are really best for this dish). Sprinkle with salt and dip in cornmeal until covered. Fry in a little butter until a nice brown. Cover the frying pan throughout the cooking process to keep the tomatoes tender. Serve either plain or with a brown sauce.

BELL PEPPER (FRED HARVEY STYLE)

Six skinned bell peppers (enough to make twelve orders); two to three onions; three ounces of butter or olive oil; one green pepper; a tablespoon of flour; one crushed clove of garlic; three or four egg plants [*sic*]; two whole eggs; one half-pint of milk; a handful of fresh bread crumbs. Remove the skin from the peppers by dipping them into hot grease. Peel the egg plant [*sic*] and cut in dice a quarter of an inch thick. Cut the peppers in two lengthwise, remove the fleshy part adhering to the seeds, chop it and add to the egg plant [*sic*]. Cut the onions and green peppers fine; put on the fire with oil or butter and let cook for ten minutes. Add the crumbs, garlic, egg plant [*sic*], a little salt and stir frequently until done. Add the flour; mix well; pour in the milk; let come to a boil and keep stirring. Add the eggs and a little chopped parsley. Mix well, season if necessary and remove from the fire. Stuff the bell peppers with this mixture. Sprinkle with grated cheese; put a small lump of butter on each one and leave them in a hot oven long enough to produce a nice golden brown.

Chicken a la King

Take the breasts of tender fowls, slice in size desired. Let simmer in fresh butter a while. Add for one fowl two gills (one-half pint) of sherry wine; one small cupful of cream. Season to taste. Beat together four yolks of eggs and a quarter cupful of cream. Parboil and dice one green pepper, one sweet pepper; slice four mushrooms. Mix all ingredients together.

Mackerel Baked in Cream

Skin, bone and divide a large fish into four pieces, season and fry in butter, drain it and put the pan where it will keep hot. Mix half a pint of white stock, or Bechamel sauce, with the yolk of an egg, stir over the fire for a minute or two, pour over the fish and put chopped parsley and onions and breadcrumbs over the top of the fish.

Lamb Chops a la Nelson

Make a dressing of boiled onions and grated cheese, passing through a sieve; broil chop on one side only, cover the unbroiled side with dressing and place in hot oven to brown; garnish with tongue tips and mushroom tops.

German Potato Salad

Boil twelve potatoes. While hot cut in thin slices, cover with finely sliced onions and add one teaspoonful of salt and one half-teaspoonful of pepper. Mix the yolk of one egg with three tablespoonsful of olive oil and four tablespoonsful of vinegar. Pour the well-mixed dressing over the potatoes, then pour a half-cupful of boiling water or broth over the whole mixture and stir well. Sprinkle with chopped parsley; cover and let stand for a few hours. This salad never will be dry.

Cocoanut [*sic*] Bars

Five whites of eggs beaten very stiff; add ten ounces of granulated sugar, seven ounces of cocoanut [*sic*]; mix together, spread on wafer paper and cut in finger shapes. Place on buttered pans and bake in a cool oven.

Rice Pudding

Wash and boil two tablespoonsful of rice in water to cover. Dissolve a quarter of a boxful of gelatin in cold water and stir into the rice while hot. Allow this to cool, then add a cupful of sugar, two tablespoonsful of chopped, preserved figs. Put on ice several hours. Serve with whipped cream.

Banana Pie

Peel and slice the bananas thin, add sugar, a little butter and some spice, allspice or a dash of ginger, a little acid syrup, lemon or orange juice. Bake with full cover or put on a meringue when done. Another way is to make a syrup with one-half pint of water and vinegar, one pound of sugar and some allspice, and season the bananas with the syrup.

CRANBERRY SHERBET

Place one quart of cranberries in three cups of boiling water and let boil about ten minutes. When the berries are well softened, strain through a sieve. Let one and one-half cupsful of sugar, in one quart of water, boil twenty minutes. Add one tablespoonful of gelatin that has been soaked in two tablespoons of cold water. When cool, strain and add the cranberries, with more sugar if desired. Then freeze as usual.

FRENCH APPLE PIE WITH NUTMEG SAUCE

Eight cups sliced, tart apples; one-half cup water; one and one-half cups sugar; one recipe plain pastry; one cup all-purpose flour; one-half cup sugar; one-third cup butter; one cup graham crackers crushed; few drops of vanilla. For sauce mix one egg yolk; one-half cup sugar; one cup milk. Heat to the boiling point; remove from heat and add nutmeg. Cook apples in water until tender; add sugar and mix carefully to retain shape of apples. Arrange apples in pastry lined pie plate. Combine graham cracker crumbs, flour, sugar, butter and vanilla. Mix until it resembles coarse crumbs, sprinkle mixture over apples. Bake in hot oven ten minutes, then in moderate oven twenty minutes.
Serve with Nutmeg Sauce.

SOME PRACTICAL SUGGESTIONS

To preserve the natural sweetness, color and flavor of green peas, cook them in their shells. Put them in a steamer until they are done. It will take two-thirds less time to shell them than when raw, and they will require but very little seasoning.

Corn on the cob is cooked to perfection by putting it in a steamer, dry, for twenty minutes with a moderate steam. Then dip the ears into a pan containing hot water, milk and salt, and they will be ready to serve.

Potatoes baked in their skins always will come out more dry and mealy if a small piece is cut off one end to allow the steam to escape in the cooking.

Green vegetables should be boiled fast, with a pinch of carbonate of soda, with the sauce-pan lid off.

Jelly should not be put into the mold until it is on the point of setting. If this rule is observed there never will be any difficulty in turning out the most delicate cream, jelly or aspic.

Appendix II
ADDITIONAL SOURCES

NAME	HARVEY HOUSE RELATIONSHIP	METHOD OF COMMUNICATION
Adams, Evelyn	Harvey Girl, Brownwood, Texas	personal interview
Balke, James	son of Casper Balke, Harvey House busboy, Somerville, Texas; nephew of Adeline Balke, Harvey Girl, Somerville, Texas	personal correspondence
Bell, Mary E.; Bishop, Lorene; Drinkard, Alene	Harvey House, Brownwood, Texas	narrative history
Bratcher, Ann Wessels	daughter of Zadie Wessels, Harvey Girl, Houston, Texas, and John Wessels, Harvey House chef, Houston, Texas, and Deming, New Mexico	personal interview
Dehrkoop, Pres	historian, Harvey Girls of El Paso, Texas	personal interview and correspondence

NAME	HARVEY HOUSE RELATIONSHIP	METHOD OF COMMUNICATION
Ellis, Bessie Mae "Bunk"	daughter of Lillian Preas, Harvey Girl, Brownwood, Texas	personal interview
Farschon, Rose	Harvey Girl, Slaton, Texas	personal interview and correspondence
Flynn, Dorothy	friend of Jewell Curtis, Harvey Girl, Cleburne, Texas	personal correspondence
Fondy, Jolene	daughter of Ethel Reeves, Harvey Girl, Sweetwater, Texas, and Joe Tate, Harvey House busboy, Slaton Texas	personal interview
Gaut, C. Rufus	collection of information relating to the Santa Fe Orchestra, Amarillo, Texas	telephone interview and correspondence
Hines, Keith	Santa Fe Railroad employee	personal correspondence
Johnson, Erna Koen	Harvey Girl, Temple, Texas	personal interview and correspondence
Johnson, Maxine Cockrell	Harvey Girl, Canadian, Texas	personal correspondence
Jordan, Desree Arrowood	Harvey Girl, Amarillo, Texas, Waynoka, Oklahoma, Dodge City, Emporia and Newton, Kansas	personal correspondence
Kiddney, Patricia Bevel	historian, Harvey Girls of El Paso, Texas	personal interviews and correspondence
King, Grace	niece of historian and radio personality Mary Robertson Hudgins, KXOX Radio, Sweetwater, Texas	script of museum segment of *Coffee Show*, May 1994

NAME	HARVEY HOUSE RELATIONSHIP	METHOD OF COMMUNICATION
Lamb, Calvin	Harvey House busboy, Slaton, Texas	telephone interview
Moore, Leona Woods	Harvey Girl, Temple, Slaton, Brownwood, Somerville, Texas and the Grand Canyon	personal correspondence
Newton, Ruth Norville	Harvey Girl, Temple, Cleburne, Sweetwater, Brownwood and Houston, Texas	personal correspondence
Nichols, Raymond	pantry boy, Cleburne, Texas	personal correspondence
Phillips, Dana G.	daughter of Etta Lanham Williams, Harvey Girl, Temple, Texas	personal correspondence
Preas, Lillian	Harvey Girl, Brownwood, Texas	personal interview and correspondence
Saenz, Madge	Harvey Girl, Galveston, Texas	personal and telephone interview, personal correspondence
Saenz, Raymond	son of Madge Jones Saenz, Harvey Girl, Galveston, Texas	personal correspondence
Schurig, Rudolph G.	son of Ernest Emil Schurig, Harvey House chef and baker, Gainesville, Texas	personal correspondence
Slaughter, Jacky	granddaughter of Kelpie Ann Rainy, Harvey Girl, El Paso, Texas	telephone interview
Smith, Alma Vera Allen	Harvey Girl, Canadian, Texas	personal correspondence

NAME	HARVEY HOUSE RELATIONSHIP	METHOD OF COMMUNICATION
Southwest Collection, Texas Tech University, Lubbock, Texas	Fannie Green Teague, Harvey Girl, Vaughn, New Mexico, and Slaton, Texas	recorded interview conducted by David Murrah
Stine, Edith	niece of Carl Webber, Harvey Hotel manager, Amarillo, Texas	personal correspondence
Strawn, Ruth Wilson	daughter of Charles Everett Wilson, Harvey House Cook, Cleburne, Texas	personal correspondence
Weaver, Pat	friend of Alice Garnas, Harvey Girl, Canadian, Texas	personal correspondence
Wilson, Spec	son of Maxine Cockrell Wilson Johnson, Harvey Girl, Canadian, Texas	personal correspondence
Woods, B.H.	brother of Leona Woods, Harvey Girl, Somerville, Texas	personal correspondence

BIBLIOGRAPHY

Armstrong, William Patrick. *Fred Harvey Creator of Western Hospitality.* Bellemont, AZ: Canyonlands Publications, 2000.

Bryant, Keith L. *History of the Atchison, Topeka and Santa Fe Railway.* New York: Macmillan Publishing Company, Inc., 1974.

Foster, George H., and Peter C. Weiglin. *The Harvey House Cookbook.* Atlanta: Longstreet Press, 1992.

Fried, Stephen. *Appetite for America: Fred Harvey and the Business of Civilizing the Wild West—One Meal at a Time.* New York: Random House, Inc., 2010.

Grattan, Virginia L. *Mary Colter: Builder upon the Red Earth.* Flagstaff, AZ: Northland Press, 1980.

Henderson, James D. *Meals by Fred Harvey: A Phenomenon of the American West.* Fort Worth: Texas Christian University Press, 1969.

Landrey, Wanda A. *Boardin' in the Thicket.* Denton: University of North Texas Press, 1990.

Marshall, James. *Santa Fe: The Railroad That Built an Empire.* New York: Random House, 1945.

Mims, Mollie Gallop Bradbury. *Johnson County History Book.* Dallas, TX: Curtis Media, 1985.

Poling-Kempes, Lesley. *The Harvey Girls: Women Who Opened the West.* New York: Paragon House, 1989.

Waters, L.L. *Steel Trails to Santa Fe.* Lawrence: University of Kansas Press, 1950.

INDEX

S

Saenz, Madge 45, 84, 85, 87, 88
Santa Fe Magazine 19, 36, 47, 72, 100
Santa Fe, New Mexico 88
Santa Fe Orchestra, Amarillo, Texas 52
Schluens, John 41
Schurig, Ernest Emil 40
Scrofine, Johnny 87
Sells, Opal 49, 50
Silsbee, Texas 44, 45, 47
Slaton, Texas 13, 43, 62, 63, 65, 67, 68, 69, 70, 87, 127
Slaughter, Jacky 93
Smith, Alma Vera Allen 56
Smith, Willard 52
Somerville News Tribune 41
Somerville, Texas 36, 40, 41, 42, 43, 44, 45
Spindletop oil boom 102
Stamford, Texas 83
Steele, Marshall 57
Strawn, Ruth Wilson 31
Strickland, Nello 43
Studley Hazel 34
Sweetwater, Texas 13, 59, 60, 61, 62, 63, 108

T

Tate, Joe 62
Teague, Fannie Belle Green 63, 65, 67
Temple Daily Telegram 38
Temple, Texas 23, 34, 36, 38, 43, 47
  Dairy 36, 43
Thomas, Robert Otis 45, 60, 88
Tolzien, Irving 52
Topeka, Kansas 23, 54, 72

V

Vaughn, New Mexico 32, 63

W

Wayne King Orchestra 43
Waynoka, Oklahoma 50
Weber, C.W. 51
Wessels, John 98
Wessels, Zadie 98
White, Ella 43
Williams, Etta Lanham 37
Wilson, Charles Everett 31
Wilson, Harold 55
Wolf, Cleo 67, 68
Wolf, Irene 67
Woods, Leona 43
Worsham, Laura and Sidney 34

X

Xanterra 24

ABOUT THE AUTHOR

Author Rosa Walston Latimer.
Photo by Mary Stevenson Norman.

R osa Walston Latimer owns an independent bookstore and is a playwright and an award-winning photographer. She has written for national and regional magazines and newspapers and was news editor of a print and an online newspaper and supervising director of a nationally syndicated television program.

The story of her Harvey Girl grandmother sparked her interest in preserving women's history. After being told by a museum curator in another state that there were no Harvey Houses in Texas, she was determined to preserve this important part of the state's railroad history and inspired to write her first book, *Harvey Houses of Texas: Historic Hospitality from the Gulf Coast to the Panhandle.*

Rosa first wrote about Texas Harvey Houses in an article for *Texas Highways*. Later, she wrote a play, *The Harvey Girls*, based on the true story of how her grandmother and grandfather met at a Harvey House. Two of the ten performances of the play were in the original lunchroom of the restored Harvey House in Slaton, Texas.

Rosa lives above her bookstore in a two-story, historic building. She shares the upstairs space with her three rescue dogs: Muffin, Penny and Ally. Downstairs, the bookstore cat, Ruby, happily greets customers and watches the traffic on Main Street. Rosa is actively involved in the arts and historical preservation of her community, and gallery space in the store features regional artists. She is currently writing a play about women who were the real "Rosie the Riveters" and researching a book about female ranchers. She also plans to develop a fictional series about Harvey Girls.